Exploring Spirituality
in Photo & Verse

by Arlene Goetze

Art by JoAnne Arnold

Copyright 2020 by Arlene Goetze

All prose and poetry in this book is written by Arlene Goetze except quotes or short song lines with their authors named. All photographs were taken by Arlene Goetze except for several by family members.

All rights reserved. No part of this book may be used or reproduced in any manner whatsoever, except in the case of reprints in the context of reviews, without written permission from the author.

Paperback ISBN: 978-0-578-73971-7

Arlene Goetze, Publisher

Printed in the United States of America

Acknowledgements

Some 10,000 plus readers followed my writings in ***Catholic Women's Network*** newspaper (1989-2005). Two dozen women wrote columns and three drew cartoons. It is with their unknowing encouragement that ***Exploring Spirituality in Photo & Verse*** becomes my tenth book in print.

The helping hands have changed with each book, but for this book, I give thanks to those spiritual beings who appear in these 65 *Photo Reflections*, who inspire virtues even in ice-cream cones or planting pumpkin seeds. I'm grateful some family members gave me several of the photos in this book to inspire spirituality along with some from the thousands I have taken over 40 years' time.

JoAnne Arnold, an artist friend for some 40 years, prepared logo of path stones. Math professor Rosalee Clarke and spiritual director Suzanne Young used the red pencil as proofreaders, and family members, Ryan Meth, Thomas Goetze, and Ann Reigelman, educated me in updated computer publishing skills. My husband Earl keeps my complicated computer equipment storing some 40 years of articles, satires, meditations, and poetry organized for present use.

Do enjoy the loving deer in one photo who bless you with spiritual peace and serenity.

Dedication

to my mother,
Catherine A. Gowinski
(nee Budinski)
who taught me that common sense
and two years of schooling was all
she needed to solve all problems
during her 102 years of life.

Contents

Photos . . . On the Way 1
Meditation: On the Way 2

I. **Innocence: Virtues and Values in Children** 3
    Value of Curiosity 4
    Value of Touch 6
    Virtue of Trust 8
    Spirituality of Pleasure 10
    Value of Helpfulness 12
    Virtue of Docility 14
    Value of Auras 16
    Virtue of Respect 18
    Meditation: Holy Air 20
    Virtue of Courage 22
    Value of Insight 24
    Value of Imagination 26
    Value of Reflection 28

II. **The Ordinary: Spirituality in Everyday Actions** 31
    Spirituality of the Apple 32
    Conversation 34
    Food Shopping 36
    Planting 38
    Spirituality of Exercise 40
    Spirituality of Clothing 42
    Graduation 44
    Spirituality of Light 46

III. **Bare Necessities: Hands and Feet** 49
    Bless these Hands 50
    Holding Hands 52
    Palming 54
    Sculpting 56
    Cavewriting 58
    Playing 60
    Swimming 62
    Feeding 64
    Blessed Earth 66
    Foot History 68
    Walking/Running 70
    Stretching 72
    Dancing 74
    Orchestra of Feet 76
    Boots 78
    Shoes 80

IV Pray-ers: Actions for the Spirit 83

Connect with Soul 84	An Altar/Shrine 96
Candles 86	Holy Water 98
Holy Fire 88	Clowning 100
Music 90	Stringing Along 102
Statues 92	Labyrinth 104
Rocks 94	Body, Mind, Soul 106

V Memories: Recording a Spiritual Life 109

Recording the Spiritual 110	Healing Drums 130
Purrfect Memories 112	Spirit of Laughter 132
A Son's Spirit 114	Spirit of Ancestors 134
Threads of Wisdom 116	Of Silence and Sound 136
Women's Circle 118	On our Way 137
The Woman 120	Letter of Goodbye 138
The Holy Oak 122	Publications by Arlene
Spirit of a Tree 124	Goetze 140
Graceful Art of Dying 126	The Author 141
A Spiritual Will 128	

Photos . . . On the Way

Gently I step
cautiously toeing the
unseen jags along the way.
I balance
landing firm on the
flagstones of spiritual growth.
Open to maturity
my pathway to authenticity
is innocent.
What will I see!

Meditation: On the Way

*Bare your feet on this journey for a trip into the unknown.
Clear your mind of chatter and breathe deeply of Holy Air.*

Take your first step on the trail of truth, balancing firmly
with both feet bare, feeling the smooth slate and sturdiness
of the rocks on which you stand.

Step gently on the stones of strength, absorbing earth energy,
fortifying body, mind, and spirit for the way ahead.
Soak in the life force of divine power.

Slip smoothly on the gems of justice, grasping their glitter as they
catch the light of sun and glimmer of the moon.
Curl your feet to grip the stones like the precious jewels they are.

Parade along your path of peace, caressing small pebbles with
your toes, soaking calm from harmony and balance.
Feel serene and tranquil on your way.

Be light-footed on the curving lane of love leading you to
levels of new life. Step into the clouds of joy and ecstasy
as you float in the warmth of everlasting love.

*May we all tread the path of truth
step firmly on the stones of strength
jog hard for the cause of justice
parade proudly on the path of peace
and be passionate in our sharing of love.*

---

*In early Christian times, people were known as people
On the Way, on a spiritual journey.
We join them on our path to our own Spirit.*

I. Innocence

This is a book about spirituality, so at the beginning, we start at the beginning of life. Look in the eyes of some of the babies in this first section called "Innocence."

What do you see in the eyes of the baby in the crib on page 5?
Surprise?   Awareness?   Security?   Curiosity?

What does the little fairy with wings on page 15 express?
Concern over what to do? Thoughts about flying?

Definitions of innocence in dictionaries speak of purity, goodness, freedom from guilt, or evil. Characteristics of innocence in psychology or fiction include integrity and compassion, courage and love, and even silence and humility.

Humor is a definite spiritual quality of this state in life—babies laugh often at what they do not understand. Those older but with slower mental abilities retain their innocence; and elders, losing memories with age, once again may show the innocence of the young. The developed mind is involved.

This book fits in spiritual journeys for people of many ages--on different levels of spiritual growth. Our photos move into a spiritual space which can be considered to be a "movement of authenticity of the soul."

Come, share the journey in this book of Spiritual Smiles but you are on a spiritual journey in all stages of life.

We offer a menu of humor, insight, and wisdom.

Arlene Goetze, Editor/Writer/Photographer/Poet

Value of Curiosity

Curiosity is often quoted as being the downfall of cats, but it actually is the making of humans as the desire to know or learn something. Our baby in the crib uses her eyes of wonder to be open to what comes next in her physical life.

Now content with the simple pleasure of her pacifier and the safety of her crib, she stares into the present to be open to the future. She knows little else in her first few months of life beside these comforts.

She is a picture of curiosity . . . her alert eyes show a willingness to learn what goes on in the bigger world. She is open to the path of wisdom in her life although she is innocent of what that might mean.

Wisdom is an inborn but undeveloped quality in the soul which guides the body into ethics and morality in physical life. It is a movement toward authenticity, of learning the basics of faith, hope, love, peace, patience, and understanding. It pushes one to develop the soul along with the body.

In spiritual practices like meditation, positive thinking, and yoga, both the body and mind can be open to the growth of many qualities which are reflected in the photos in this book.

We start with a reflection of how both virtues and values reflect the innocence of our babies, children, and animals.

Curiosity

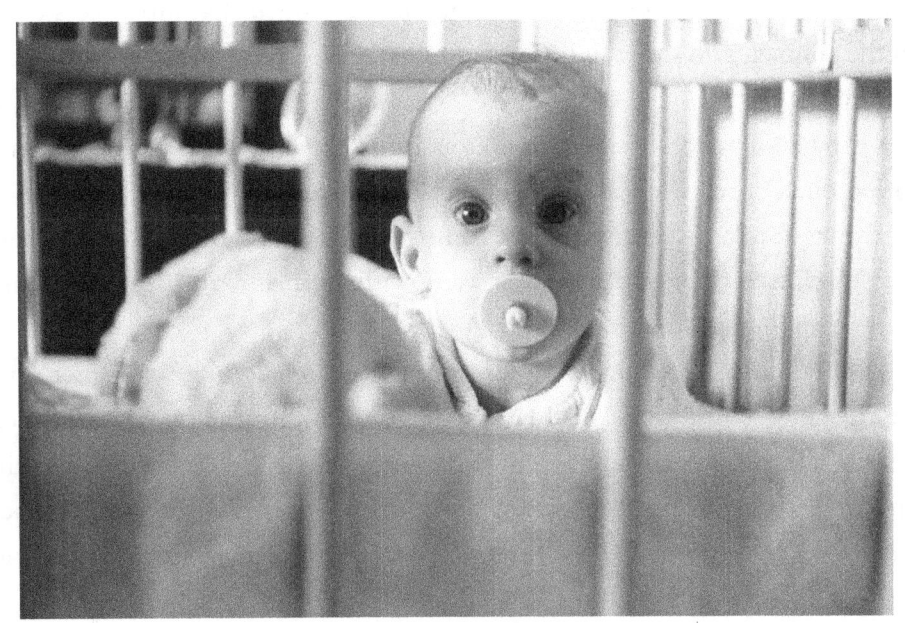

What? Time to wake up?
I'm so comfy here . . .
listening . . . seeing . . . snuggling
in the softness
secure within the bars that
keep me safe from harm.

What? Stand up? Speak out?
Climb out into the space that has
no bounds
where open doors invite discovery.
Is that why I was born?

Value of Touch

How does one touch the untouchable Spirit of the Divine? Our baby girl is content feeling successful in touching a baby boy whose eyes reflect surprise. Both are innocent of the value of their touch that introduces them to the contact with other living creatures as well as the power of the Supreme Creator.

She does not realize her strong touch to keep herself from falling over is like a touch of reiki, a healing art that restores health in bodies. He, receiving a healing touch, is surprised at the feelings he has of keeping his own stability. As with reiki, energy moves in each of them, bringing a form of divine change neither understands.

Our sense of touch is always working. It opens us to a higher level we do not often understand but which has meaning for earthly existence. Touch can open us to finding the authenticity we need to become healthy and whole. It is the first sense a newborn infant feels and often the last touch a loved one receives at death. The value of touching is a gift from the Divine.

A Short Reflection

Choose a sacred object that symbolizes Spirit or the Divine, something small enough to comfortably fit in your hand.

With your eyes closed, feel the object, exploring it with your fingers. What words define how it feels?

In what ways does this mirror your inability to actually touch something untouchable?

Now go outside and notice textures all around you. Rough, smooth, cold? Which textures remind you of something divine? Which are the opposite?

As you take a deep breath, what do you touch that reminds you that you also have a Divine nature? That you are also a holy one?

With every deep breath today, remember how you are divine—how the physical can facilitate touching the spiritual.

Touch

I've got him. He's mine.
He looks so strong and neat.

But I'm not up for grabs
I'm not yet on my feet.

Virtue of Trust

One of my early memories is recorded in a snapshot of my toddler body hiding behind my mother's long skirt. My early life was shaky enough for me to cling to the skirts of someone I knew.

Trust is inherent in the feeling of safety. In this photo the toddler girl, still wobbly in her walking, leans on her mother and hangs on her hair. Still with a thumb for comfort, she begins the virtue of trust, the first step in awakening her spirituality.

We learn to trust ourselves when we learn to trust others. The more trust she has, the sooner she will progress leaning on herself and walking alone. This is the awakening of the soul into trusting the world beyond and especially the existence of the divine world. Listening is a key factor in trust development.

Here the child listens as the mother herself is in a listening mode. Spirituality does not arise in us like a thunder bolt but more like a gentle rain in tiny drops. Our current five-year old cat, with feral beginnings, still lacks the ability to trust people or places. She is frightened when company comes, and she eyes the backyard with great fright before entering it. She doesn't seem to trust the food we give her is healthy.

Trust indeed is a most important virtue to develop in infancy. Without it, the world lacks security for peace and love, both physical and divine. It is the warm arms of mom or dad, holding and hugging, rocking and touching their baby that gives them the gift of trust.

Trust

I taste the sweet security
of my thumb
sucking, drawing on the comfort of my flesh
connecting with the body
wherein I live.
Leaning on my mother
I grab her tangled hair
to steady myself pushing, pulling, testing
She is solid. Trust begins!

Spirituality of Pleasure

This photo was taken in the 1970s when African-Americans were finally free to eat ice cream in public with German-Americans. During pre-school years, these toddlers had the pleasure of eating ice cream together, playing in beach sand at a retreat house, and sharing meals in a family spirituality group.

Each was the youngest of seven in their military families. Fourteen years before this, the older sister/brother of these two were not allowed in some states to eat in pubic together. Can the eyes of these babies see what is coming in their future?

Although there were 24 flavors of ice cream then, vanilla and chocolate were favorites. With some dozens of skin colors today, vanilla and chocolate have blended. So what does the color of skin have to do with spirituality or ice cream?

It is not the color of skin but the healthy condition of skin that is the focus of spirituality. Shamans long ago and today offer spiritual healing to cure those with leprosy, acne, rashes, and other skin problems. Natural healing methods work on these physical issues today.

Auras, the mysterious glow around people of all skin colors, can indicate a spiritual component. Like angel halos, that light emitted is a form of energy. Toddlers and ice-cream mean innocent pleasure on a warm afternoon. This alone is pleasure for the spirit.

Pleasure

Vanilla or chocolate
the ice-cream clerk asks
Why must I choose?

Marble I answer
blending he two
Spirituality makes no choice!

Value of Helpfulness

This toddler and teen are playing the game of brushing hair, a common skill toddlers like to develop. Teens as a subject are more fun than a doll with curls.

Lending a hand is a phrase not yet known to this toddler, but lend a hand she does. With her own hair too short for tangles, she practices the art of brushing on very long snarled hair its owner cannot reach. She may recognize a need to help another but also to help herself in learning a task. Helpfulness is a step toward cooperation which reveals spiritual qualities of understanding and goodness as well as care for others.

This child could also practice this art of brushing on a doll or animal. While she is learning a task, she can practice on a toy or give affection to a cat or dog who craves it and who will give her gratitude in their own way.

When we give food to the hungry or a home to the homeless, we develop a spiritual quality which brings us to a higher level of consciousness where our spirituality can develop.

A Haircut

As I wait my turn the fifth in line and watch a baby smiling fine
the customers in this hair cuttery await the stylists who are fluttery.
They chat and giggle with each other in a foreign language mutter.
They ring their sale, then look at you, ready for the next hairdo.

Under plastic tent and tissued neck, I feel the snip of shears by heck.
Clips of gray hair fill my lap; my eyes are closed I start to nap.
Relaxing with the gentle touch that revs my brain so very much,
my time is up, my hair is shorn--a simple haircut, I'm reborn.

Helpfulness

Tangles and snarls, oh I've made a mess
but I've got a brush which I must confess
will smooth out the knots with nary a tug.
This brush it is magic, it can smooth like a hug.

It will give you a hairdo with beauty and shine.
Your tresses will fall exactly in line.
The bristles know how to make this all well
so your hairstyle will look really swell!

Virtue of Docility

Even at this tender age, the tiny winged angel knows her wings don't fly. As she ponders her instructions from above to fly, she stands rooted in the ground.

This little-known virtue of docility is a humble readiness to follow a Divine will in our lives. Here this young earthbound angel is listening to the 'divine' instruction of her holy mother to move her along her spiritual path. The advice she gets may not be perfect since flying is beyond her body; and it may not be what she needs for Halloween, the reason for her costume, but she is willing to try.

Docility does involve spiritual advice because it must be stimulated by something outside itself to grow. One must be willing to move in directions suggested by others to learn more of the spiritual side of oneself. Flying may not take this angel's body into heavenly space, but it can challenge her prayerful imagination into flying behind the clouds to find a friendship with the Divine.

Illumination through Virtue

Light up, light up my inner self
I ask my cells to shine.
Glow forth, illuminate
my body's spiritual state.
Am I kind enough or thoughtful?
Do I give enough of what I have?
Is virtue resting much too long?
Has it slowed my inner song?
Today I'll practice all my manners
kind and patient as one can be.
I'll light up like the northern star
you can see me sparkle afar.

Docility

Try! Holy mommy says. Try!
Whoosh your wings and fly.
Sip life's sweet nectar,
savor the passion of its fruit.
Pass on the pollen, sprinkle the dust
as you flutter toward future life.
Fly! Holy mommy says. Fly!
Whoosh your wings and fly.
I guess I'll try.

Value of Auras

Let my little light shine! We are familiar with halos perched around the heads of angels, but lights glowing around human bodies have another name. An aura is a ray of light around a person.

One belief is that an aura is an energy field which can appear in many colors, reflecting the person's state of health. Some consider it a form of electricity. Cameras often pick up auras not seen by most eyes. I often see auras in circles of blue, green, and white around the moon. When I see people with a dark background behind them, I can see auras as they are reflected in this photo.

It was at a family wedding that this young couple's energy lighted up the dance floor in 1998. Can these cousins be soulmates?

Auras

When earth first stepped beyond the water
into a world with moon and stars
there was this strange new thing called light
when sun smiled making dark so bright.
Around each plant and mammal growing
an aura started to appear,
light coming from each object present
swimming fish or flying pheasant.
Now some million years have passed
and auras flow both in and out.
My body has its rays of sunshine
helping me to glow just fine.

Auras

Ain't she sweet, swaying on her feet?
Now I ask you very confidentially, ain't she sweet?
    Ain't he smooth, dancing in a groove?
    Now I ask you very confidentially, ain't he smooth?

    We tap our feet, marking a rhythm of life.
        Can we dance in step?
Our heads are spinning, twirling our auras when we meet.
        Are we two-in-one?
Our souls are stirring, strumming the strings of our hearts.
        Are we too young to be soulmates?

Virtue of Respect

Oscar, a cat now five-years old in a Rhode Island hospital, is reported to have predicted correctly the death of some 50 hospital patients. He goes to the bed of the dying, cuddling near the patient until death, and then moving on to another. Nurses often put the cat near one they believe dying, but Oscar often moves on, proving more accurate in his choice of whom to soothe.

Our current cat who was deserted by one family, now gets very edgy when my husband packs a suitcase for a trip. She knows he's leaving. She copies the way we clean her potty box by putting waste into a plastic sack. She now pulls a plastic sack into her box to defecate on and make my cleaning easier.

Animals are now revealing more emotions and understanding besides just suffering and joy. Elephants show respect for their elders, monkeys are nice to their neighbors, cats and dogs sense human feelings, and one lonely swan, without a partner, fell in love with a tractor.

Respect is a virtue that treats all living things with honor. It is a right of every creature to have its unique positive life force be recognized and treated with kindness. So how does an innocent child have this ability in toddlerhood and the adult sheep in maturity?

This photo reveals a balance of power and energy between the two. The bewildered child stands with her own power while going nose-to-nose with a curious sheep. She works beyond her fear, and the sheep rewards her with its patience. Together they share an experience helping them both succeed in moving along an uphill path of spiritual essence, unique to each.

Respect

Oh sheep I am bewildered
by strange creatures in this land.
I'm overwhelmed with sights and sounds
that I don't understand.
I wonder if I trust in spirit
and look things in the face
that we can learn to get along
in this same earthly place.
We each have rights we must respect
to fill our world with kindness.
I do respect that you are sheep
and I am shepherdess!

Meditation: Holy Air

Place an object in front of you that reminds you of air: a feather, a steam of ribbons. Perhaps turn on a fan to feel moving air.

Breathe in deeply, filling your lungs with air. Imagine the Divine filling each cell in your body and rushing through your veins.
This is holy air. We breath holy air.
Breathe out slowly. Let your breath blow a kiss, release tension and stress, send out your goodness to be inhaled by others.
This is holy air. Our breath is holy.
Feel yourself like a feather, fluttering along on wafts of air. Let air nudge you out of melancholy into joy, out of confusion into calm.
Flutter along on the breath of the Divine.
Be still in the silence of night. Listen to the sound of air – beyond the passing car, the plane overhead, the barking dog.
Breathe deeply of the silence of holy air.
Envision yourself on a boat at sea. The wind massages your hair. You face the wind with courage, bravery, and faith.
Grow strong on the Divine wind.
Prepare for the tornado of the Divine. Rage with the winds of injustice. Blow the gates of prejudice. Level the houses of hate.
Move with the energy of Divine breath.

Prayer

Divine air, I inhale you with every breath, nurturing every cell.
Let me breathe your holy air.
God of the silence, I listen for your voice and rhythm of life.
Let me hear your voice in the silent waves of holy air.
Divine powerful wind, I am strong, facing faith. tests of courage.
Let me stand strong as I sail through the waters of life.
Divine raging tornado, I stand in awe of your message.
Energize me with your power of action and compassion.
I am filled with holy air.

Holy Air

Your cool air blows on high
breezing through my brain.
Your whirr swims in each cell
making a soft refrain.
I blow my energy at you
I too can alter air.
We each have power to change
we just make one grand pair!

Virtue of Courage

There is more to courage than going to war or jumping from an airplane. Courage comes when we step beyond innocence to test what may cause us a certain level of fear.

One of our sons was born with facial deformities. After his first surgery at four months, he was placed on his face which ripped out the surgery and required a blood transfusion. I learned never leave a child alone in a hospital.

When this son was four and in the best military hospital in the country, I refused to leave him unattended all night. In a ward of a dozen small children, some parents were smoking at an oxygen tent, and aides were yelling at babies crying without parent company. I was threatened with the Military Police if I did not leave. I found the courage to explain the situation to a doctor, and the unhealthy conditions in the ward were changed.

When we follow a spiritual heart, we can gain self-confidence that moves us along a spiritual path to a higher level of living. Sometimes this new experience leads to new friends or hobbies or occupations. It led to the safety of my son who had many surgeries where I wouldn't leave him alone.

Courage is one of six core virtues considered the foundation of human strengths and virtues. It requires that one go deep inside with meditation or contemplation. It helps one step beyond the past with self-confidence and an inner strength to try something new to move onto a new relation with the Divine. It is the needed push to follow desires of the heart and mind with new experiences.

Two young children in this photo truly demonstrate the simple courage of learning the friendly art of dancing.

Courage

I wonder if she'll dance with me . . .
I don't know how to ask.
        I wonder what. he has in mind
        He's sweating at the task.

We're holding hands and leading off,
we're holding on so tight.
        Our hands move first and then our feet
        We want to get this right.

Value of Insight

Can our faces reveal when we get an insight? Can we call it an awakening? Or enlightenment?

If we see without insight then we lack understanding, so we don't see the meaning at all. Our physical eye may be good, but our inward eye is blind so we don't perceive the reality.

A family wedding, where there were many flower girls wearing the same dress, demonstrated that insight does have an exterior display. All the girls were dressed alike which shows on the face of one four-year old. Four facial photos reveal surprise, recognition of meaning, thought, and acceptance of being dressed like others. A true case of enlightenment or a spiritual awakening.

Like a butterfly coming forth from its cocoon, she has a moment of transformation to higher consciousness. That is spirituality well beyond her years.

What to Wear

Each day I puzzle over what to wear
what colors should my body bear
the lightness of the pale sky blue
the boldness of a rose-red hue.
Virtues come to dress me new
they spark in me a strange new view.
Wear patience, it's a holy thing
endure with calmness, cool, and poise
lock out the speed and worldly noise.
Attire yourself in simple ways
belted tight with truthful rays
and so my virtue list gives me the clue
of ways to greet each day anew.

Insight

Our dresses
Our dresses
Our dresses
are alike!

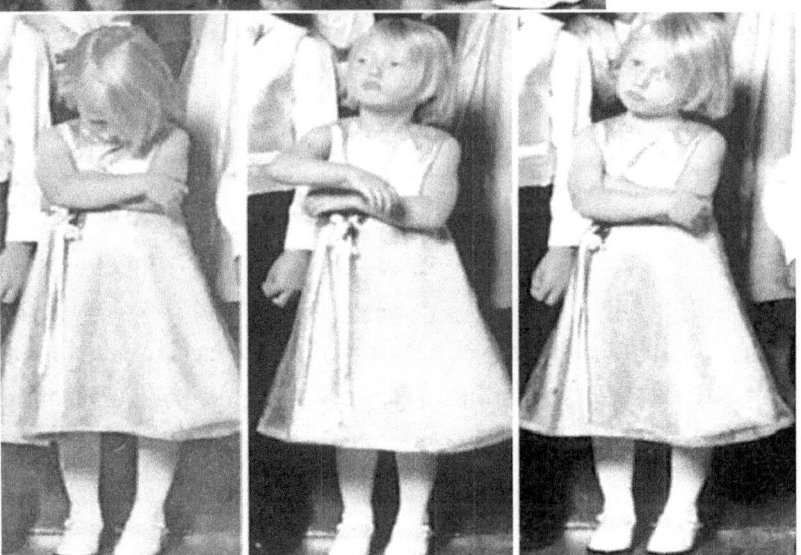

I do so want to be different, I do so want to be me.
Do you suppose, oh could it really be
that it's what inside of me that makes me so unique!

Value of Imagination

One of my daughters had a pretend friend while she was a pre-schooler. Karen was her constant companion, and when she went off to college, her roommate for four years was named Karen who has been a lifelong friend. Pretend play in our house had all seven children using their imaginations, playing as Pilgrims and cowboys, doctors and dancers with capes, crowns, and mom's old shoes.

Imagination is more than daydreaming. It is a valuable skill of creating a world beyond the reality of life. It certainly takes us outside ourselves into a space not defined by our senses or reason but full of images and symbols that urge a visible expression. Imagination can turn us from an ugly duckling into a graceful swan, and such positive play can grow us into a world of wisdom beyond our own physical reality.

Imagination should not be limited to the idea of something 'imaginary' or unreal. Everything does not have to be a result of reason and physical evidence to lead to truth. Use of our imagination opens us to the richness of our own creativity far beyond what comes from a rational philosophy.

One summer day when three granddaughters visited, they found my closet of hats and gloves. Formal white gloves with a black straw hat mixes funeral with wedding attire. A French beret caps one dreaming perhaps she is a Hollywood star.

Daydreaming, some teachers told me is a waste of time, but daydreaming was a fond occupation for me in a youth barren of travel and adventure. The reality of my hats and gloves has indeed challenged my daydreaming to positively stretch my imagination to treasured heights of a fruitful adulthood beyond any dreams I had.

Imagination

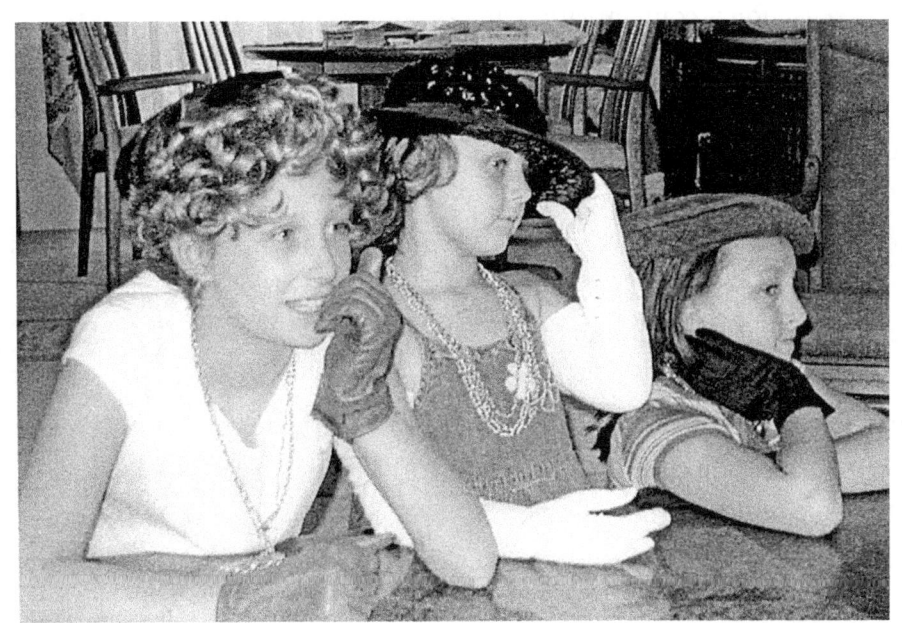

Sugar and spice and everything nice
that's what little girls are made of.
Curly locks trim and shiny black brim
pulled from the closet for dress-up day.
A French beret and white gloves gay
uplift Spirits on a long summer day.

Value of Reflection

Most of us get our first morning glimpse of ourselves by looking in the bathroom mirror. Our reflection physically is simply light bouncing off a piece of glass showing our body. But spiritual reflection means we have to go inside ourselves to brush up on our virtues and comb out the values of how we live our lives.

Reflection is contemplation or an examination of conscience as we move along the Spiritual Way. I remember one of my pre-school grandsons sitting on a tricycle in our back yard, staring at the clouds so long that I imagined he was talking with the spirit world.

A granddaughter, just turned 30, reflected to me in an email she doesn't know what to do with her life . . . though in the military, she has chased drugs ships at sea, survived the dangers in the Persian Gulf, and spent two years in the Situation Room of the White House.

My own reflections these days all seem to be in rhymes . . . whatever thought arises takes the form of simple and silly poems. Almost every virtue we reflect on can lead us to a new path, a new job, a new action in life. Reflection is truly a gift of intention, connection, and perfection of our spirits bringing joy when the mirrors we see reflect our inner souls.

Reflection

A bubble bursts inside my chest swelling joy up in my lungs.
It makes me float above the ground rising high on heaven's rungs.

I smile in my morning daydreams pulsing throbs from in my heart.
Reflection is what I call this glorious way for my day to start.

Both thoughts and images of joy freshen up my mind and soul.
Going deep inside to find myself is a path that makes me whole!

Reflection

Mirror mirror on the wall
turning my left leg to right
twinning my poor pulsing heart
as I seem to float in flight.
As I stare ahead in space
focused on my balance trick,
I hold tight my inhaled breath
until I hear the camera click.

II The ORDINARY

Julian of Norwich, a mystic writer in England in the 14th century, lived in a time of chaos and disruption, war, and the Plague. Death and suffering were everywhere, yet her writings reveal an extraordinary optimism in her abilities to find God in all things. She demonstrated that by contemplating the Divine, we can share in everlasting spiritual love.

All things shall be well. You shall see for yourself that
All manner of things shall be well. Julian of Norwich.

When we give our thoughts to the idea of Ordinary time, they usually focus on the physical, but when we meditate on the spiritual, our thoughts rise to experiences that are not visible or concrete. Yet we cannot have one without the other.

When we do see exotic places and hear outstanding music, we often try to photograph such events for future reflection. Something to capture and hold onto. It seems appropriate to name this section Ordinary because our photos are about common and often boring actions in life. We can change the ordinary into something that connects us to reverence, awe, and presence of the Divine in our lives.

Our very existence depends on our simple breath-to-breath action. We need to live in the moment if we wish to find the spiritual in our ordinary daily actions. Maybe we remember to thank God for giving us teeth when we brush them in the morning. Maybe we express gratitude when we ponder over what shirt to wear today. We can find the Divine in the gorgeous yellow blooms of the weed oxalis that overwhelm our winter yard when the rain falls in the winter.

Our photos here are from ordinary life . . . a place where we find God in every moment . . . if we take the time to look.

Spirituality of the Apple

Our spiritual journey now takes us out of the world of innocence and into the Garden of Eden where innocence is often said to turn into guilt. The mythical apple that Eve took from the Tree of Wisdom has little of a literal meaning, although in various religions, it is truth indeed. Until the 17th century, the word apple was used to describe most fruits except berries. Tomatoes were first called 'love apples,' while cucumbers were known as 'earth apples,' and oranges as 'golden apples.' When Adam ate the apple, myth tells us it stuck in his throat, thereby giving rise to the term 'Adam's Apple.'

Adam was one being, living in a state of bliss in the Garden. Eve was created from his rib, and when the serpent came along, she bit the apple—an act that brought conscious awareness into the Garden. Two such beings were created to cooperate in life, not compete.

Many religions hold the apple as a symbol, and when the Jews celebrate their New Year, they "eat an apple dipped in honey for a good new year."

Apples are a symbol of knowledge, immortality, temptation, and falling into sin as well as love and sexuality. They certainly have meaning as a passage into a new life of spiritual awareness and unity with the Creator.

> **Keep me as the apple of God's eye,**
> **hide me in the shadows of your wings.**
>
> Psalm 17:8

The Apple

Mother Eve took a chance
her bite sent shocks our way.
We take a chomp and chew it well
keeping doctors and ill health at bay.
A healthy fruit
an occasion of sin
what else lurks beneath its skin!
Oh Creator
Your subtle humor
befuddles me!

Spirituality of Conversation

Every afternoon when I take a daily walk through the park across the street, I say 'hello" to everyone I pass. Occasionally, I get a 'hello' in return. When I greet babies in buggies or dogs on leashes, they do seem to stare at me intently, waiting for more words, something often missing with humans these days. Cell phones now have people talking for hours to someone invisible. Actual conversations with awareness of presence, emotions, and concern are a struggle.

Conversation is a simple awareness of the moment with another person that involves an exchange of ideas, hopes, and thoughts without judging. Its qualities are many when it occurs in person. Patience, courtesy, listening, and respect are at the top of the list of beneficial qualities in conversations. Taking turns, asking questions, and being open to new ideas is critical.

Mindfulness is a spiritual component. While most talking does not focus on the spiritual in the present movement, when it does, that is a quality that spurs conversations to a higher level. When people talk about the meaning of life, the listener must pay close attention to another's stories, while the speaker ventures into self-revelation that makes her vulnerable.

Personal talking is time to share spiritual beliefs, thoughts, and actions that can elevate those involved to a deeper and more meaningful type of conversation.

Questions for Spirituality in Conversation:

What makes you feel fulfilled?
How do you find joy every day in your life?
How does someone give you comfort when you get depressed?
What is your goal in life? How do you try to achieve it?

Conversation

The stories we tell in the sunlight,
the hopes we spin at high noon
are seeds for the hungering earth
waiting to burst into bloom.
The stories we hide in our hearts,
the tears that we cry in the night
are dead for the hungering earth
which cannot make healthy this plight.
Let's tell our stories in groups
with love and kindness for all.
Each color and gender and age
can fill our earth hungry for sage.

Spirituality of Food Shopping

Spirituality, I learned, is a movement toward authenticity. So just how does food consist of spirituality? It depends on how 'authentic' the food is that we choose. 'You are what you eat' is a common reminder that food's value is more than physical, so how can spiritual practice find its way into our supermarkets!

Most of us do not need two shopping carts when we enter a market, so perhaps this young woman in our photo is shopping for a food kitchen for the homeless or politely returning carts other shoppers left in the parking lot. Our food needs . . . or perhaps our addictions and emotional **wants** . . . often direct our purchases over our actual **needs**. Yoga principles give us ideas:

- When people start Yoga, they often slim down because Mindfulness becomes part of their eating process.
- Breathe deeply and be calm when entering a store.
- Purchase foods that are fresh and free of genetic modification, pesticides, and plastic.
- Select foods in the amounts you will use and not waste.
- Reject cans, bottles, and boxes that list more than five natural ingredients or ingredients you don't know as food.
- 'Take only what you need and need only what you take.'

Remember to give thanks for whatever you buy. These actions form the spiritual life when buying and eating food.

Celery

My momma always told me celery was so good to eat
She washed and stripped each stalk from head to feet.
She smiled as she opened wide and took one great big bite
A chomping on the crispy stalk made her a joyful sight!

Food Shopping

Farmers Market

Each Saturday I walk the path
past bins of harvested ripe fruit
past stalls of veggies, dips, and nuts
the best of Mother Nature's loot.
Through blocking strollers and crowded aisles
I head back to the stall
where onions, squash, and peppers
have a price that is quite small.
I taste the peaches, pears, and plums
in toothpick-size array
Free samples are the market's prize
and best part of this day.

Spirituality of Planting

Not long ago an acquaintance called, asking if she could come to walk barefoot in our back yard. She was a single woman, presently unemployed, near retirement with no relatives, living in an apartment with no lawn. She was depressed, and her book on Earthing said walking barefoot on dirt or grass could help heal her.

Earthing simply is the practice of living in contact with the earth's natural surface or being grounded wherein the earth discharges and prevents chronic inflammation in the body. This contact has enormous health implications with chronic disease, including aging.

Our planet is alive with natural energies. Its surface pulsates with frequencies that can be absorbed by bare feet on dirt, sand, or natural fields—a fact not taught in schools or known by most of us.

The earth frequencies are waves of energy caused by motion of subatomic particles called free electrons, which give the earth surface a natural negative charge. When humans and animals are grounded, they absorb the electrons which reduce electrical imbalances in the body such as inflammation or many diseases.

The easiest way to connect with the earth is to walk barefoot 20 to 30 minutes a day directly . . . or to sit with bare feet on dirt. Dampening the ground may help conduct the electricity. Barefoot substitutes are available in the form of floor mats or bed sheets connected to the earth indoors.
Earthing by Ober, Sinatra, Zucker

Earthing ranks right up there with the discovery of penicillin.
         Ann Louise Gittleman, PhD, CNS

Earthing may be as fundamental as sunlight, air, water, and nutrients. May the Ground be with you.
         Gary Schwartz, PhD

Planting

Digging in the earth is what I like to do
although my plot of land is small
squeezed between two city driveways.
it is a lot of dirt to haul.

But it does grow gigantic things
huge pumpkins on the summer vine.
They make the neighbors passing by
yell out . . . I wish just one was mine!

Spirituality of Exercise

Gymnasiums or Mother Nature are frequent choices of sites for exercise. There is little dispute that exercise of the body is connected with exercise of the soul. Moving body parts sends blood and oxygen to the brain; and when the body feels good, it has better health and energy for doing spiritual works.

Years ago when I was young and gyms were favored spots, I was on a treadmill next to a very active man. He was sweating so profusely, his toxin drops were spraying on me. As I aged, I joined a senior center gym where two TV sets located above two weight machines were blasting my digital hearing aids to the heavens. So I knew that was not where I would develop spiritual connections.

I never met my Polish grandmother who gave birth to 11 and took in two grandchildren when her oldest daughter died of cancer . . . which made up for her two newborns who passed. She never heard of a gym in Canada where she sailed by boat in 1900, pregnant with my mom. She was a farmer's wife where exercise occurred during her occupation as cook, egg collector, butter maker, turkey plucker, and washerwoman. Yes, she knew what exercise was.

Today, yoga may be the most spiritual connection of Mother Nature type exercise since it practices mindfulness as part of muscle stretching. Digging in the dirt to plant, hanging clothes on the line, and trimming the rose bush are not often on the list of favored physical activity, but they are connections to a higher level than treading on metal. The value of such activity is spiritual indeed.

Moving the body keeps hormones in balance, reduces stress, and helps one stay grounded while walking, running, or swimming. Recently on my daily walk in the park, a baby bird fluttered on grass. He had not yet learned to fly, but we had a spiritual little talk together. I hope he found his wings.

Exercise

My mother never did this silly stuff
that makes me sadly huff and puff.
She fed the chickens and milked the cows
with barefoot feet as she knelt in rows.
She didn't know this strange machine
that make my muscles long and lean.
She did her running chased by a bull
on her many-mile walk to school.
So why do I groan and complain
when this exercise aches me with pain?
She walked her world 'til age 102
A lifelong privilege granted few.

Spirituality of Clothing

Clothing has moved from fig leaves worn by Eve to a brand of clothes called 'Spiritual Gangster' sold on websites of people who liked to surf in Los Angeles in 2019. They connect with yoga and doing good for others at a cost of $50 for a sleeveless top. The list of attire in between these two extremes of clothes is endless.

Some clothing carries spiritual words, while others can find meaning in certain types of fabric, style, and color. In my closet is a set of black pants with symbols of the seven Chakras that I used to wear in my Drumming for Health sessions in my home for years. Black absorbs energy of all colors but gives no energy by itself.

Can clothes generate energy? The seven colors of the chakra (energy) chart are said to match the energy of seven organs of the body: red stands for power at the base of the spine, orange is creative in the belly, yellow for emotions, and medium green for love as in the heart. Sky blue is for communication in the throat, dark blue for the third eye, and purple for the crown of the head.

Wearing those colors may indeed generate energy of that type. Silk and cotton, two natural fibers, are considered to emit more energy than synthetics. More loose and flowing fabric can swirl one in heavenly attire.

On the Line

Out on the clothesline aflap in the breeze
anchored securely with little wood pins,
the clean wash is drying in sweet-scented air
freshening up for someone to wear.
The task is an old one this hanging of clothes
pinching the pins to hold wet soggy hose.
'Tis better than using the dryer electric
it makes this task peaceful rather than hectic.

Clothing

Something old, something new,
something borrowed, something blue.
Like a bride I chose my clothes
taking my time shopping with pride.
Finger the fabric, check out the tags,
treasure another one's discarded rags.
Hand me up, hand me down,
thank you God
for this clothing go-round.

Spirituality of Graduation

Formal graduation ceremonies date from the 12th century in universities in Europe. It was an event to honor and bestow degrees of BA, MA, and PhD on those who achieved higher levels of study, which marked a person with higher intelligence and superiority.

The procession itself was a walk for graduates to celebrate a new place above the normal academic level of society. It marked the transformation and new status of the learned.

The custom of wearing long robes emerged when graduates wore inappropriate dress. In the 15th century, the unique hat was created using the hat base of the biretta worn by Catholic clergy and scholars and a mortarboard reflecting that used by bricklayers. The square shape copied the outline of books.

Graduation is a time to end memorization of facts and to find other sources to challenge human divinity. Students face the spirituality of authenticity finding beauty, hope, love, and faith in the divine aspect of all that lives outside books.

Enlightenment

The virtue of enlightenment fills everything around.
It bursts my seams with knowledge plus experience abounds.
The dark spot in my frontal cortex lightens, brightens up with age.
Shadows shrink within my brain as it fills itself with sage.
Emotions sift in daily air disperse in atmosphere
from blinding black to wisdom white.
Enlightenment I cheer.

Graduation

Sophia God
No more homework
no more books
no more teachers' dirty looks
free from papers, tests, and toil
free from burning midnight oil
free to risk a journey new
imbued with Wisdom.
Sophia . . . that's you!

Spirituality of Light

"Let there be light." Four simple words are praised for the Creation of the world. This strange new positive element appeared with the birth of the sun, the moon, and the stars. Now centuries after the arrival of plants, birds, animals, and humans, light is a word with innumerable definitions of hope, beauty, truth, and wisdom. It is always welcome, always positive, always good. It wipes out darkness which bears negative meanings of more vice than virtue.

Does anyone not welcome light? The photographer in a darkroom? Most of us hope for light at the end of a tunnel. We want a life after death. We want our children to wear a cap and gown of enlightenment.

Our photo here recalls the glittering lights that we put on our Christmas trees. People first put apples on trees on December 24, the feast of Adam and Eve, and Christians expanded the decor to include candles and then electric lights to proclaim that the birth of baby Jesus was the Light of the World on December 25.

The holiday tree illustrates the joy of a large star shining as a reminder that holidays bring joy and love, but also that the woman decorating carries the light she acquired through life. A Christmas tree light shines to remind all of a spiritual life beyond earth.

The Sun

The sun spreads warmth within my heart
It beams light to my soul – awaken be glad it says to me
you are a creature free and whole.
You too are light and warmth for others
energizing in helpful ways to usher them along their path
guiding them in all their days.

Light

I stretch so much to reach above
the chintzy tinsel and
garish glitter of holiday décor.
I seek to nourish myself with
the warm love
and serene simplicity
of the Creator's steady light.

III Bare Necessities: Hands and Feet

Back in 1984, Karl Rahner, a leading Catholic theologian at Marquette University, wrote about the "Spirituality of Head, Heart, Hands, and Feet." His lengthy comments had religious spirituality as its basis, and he made predictions about the future of these very physical parts of the body.

He predicted that spirituality must include all four elements, be humble and open, live with diversity, and the concept that the human is found in the divine and the divine in the human. Christian spirituality must be based on faith with its beliefs and ceremonies. *Spirituality Today, Vol. 36, No. 4 (Winter, 1984)*

Our book looks at spirituality as a 'movement toward the authentic' even if it does not include a particular religious or ethnic affiliation. A social worker I know has devoted his life to serving children in families with serious drug problems, homeless teens in the streets of San Francisco, and those with serious guardianship issues. He has left active practice of his religion behind him, but he continues to grow spirituality in caring for some of the least loved among us. His social outreach and financial sacrifice means a simple lifestyle.

In this book, our photos do involve our brains and hearts in the outreach of love of others, as well as Mother Earth with our hands and feet. Can our photos touch both our bodies and souls?

There is nothing more beautiful than a vulnerable heart in open hands

Amanda Mosher, *Better to be able to love than to be loveable*

Meditation: Bless these Hands

Take a few deep breaths. Relax with quiet music.
Now look at your hands.
Notice your palms, their lines, shape, and size.
Turn your hands over.
Massage your knuckles. Smooth your nails. Gently rub your hands together and feel their strength. Are they warm or cold?

What stories in your life have made your hands?
What is the simplest thing they do? the most difficult?
Who is the oldest person they have touched? the youngest?
What do they enjoy doing? Playing the piano? Kneading bread? Typing? Arranging hair? Rubbing a back? Holding hands?

How many ways do they reach out?
In welcome? With anger? In affection? As a sign of peace?
Who reaches for them? A crying child? A frail grandparent?
Each time our hands reach out, they offer the story of our life.
How whole-holy is the hand gestured in love?
Close this reflection time with a Prayer of Thanksgiving for hands.

Prayer

Sensitive hands of the Divine have created the world and all in it.
May my hands nudge new life into others.
With strong hands, the Divine has brought health to the suffering.
May my hands be filled with the strength of healing.
With human hands, bread and wine was blessed for the hungry.
May my hands willingly serve those who are empty.
May they do the work of heavenly hands. So be it!

Creation

In the beginning when everything was nothing
you held out your hand and blessed the emptiness.
You filled the space with dirt and air
the sun, the moon, and an apple for us.

In our daily work we hold out our arms
and manipulate your pieces to fill our earthly void—
cooking, birthing, quilting, planting, and inventing
even computing on the Apple we built for you.
Is this what you had in mind, Creator?

Holding Hands

Psychological studies have had lots of pleasure with holding hands as the subject. From the moment a baby uses its 'grasp reflex' to wrap a tiny hand around a parent's finger, the child soaks up feelings of love and security.

A husband holding the hand of his wife in labor can actually reduce her pain and ease her apprehension. In the animal kingdom, sea otters and penguins flap flippers while elephants touch with their trunks.

Even hormones add their loving effect to the touch of hands. The hormone Oxytocin is reported to lower blood pressure and have a measurable effect on the heart. It is an active practice between mother and small child, lovers of all ages, and caregivers for their patients.

When people hold hands in large groups it can strengthen a spirit joined in heavenly pursuits. It can make an outsider belong and soften the hearts and minds of people who disagree with each other. Such human contact does increase tiny steps on the path of spirituality.

> ***There's something so real about holding hands,***
> ***some kind of complex simplicity,***
> ***saying so much by doing so little.***
>
> Unknown

Holding Hands

It a touchy thing this reaching out
to hold another hand
to bond a force of love so strong
it strengthens all the land.

Could it be where two or three of us
have used our gift of touch?
The nourishment bestowed on us
exceeds our hopes so much.

Creator, are you in this crowd with us?
More than once?

Palming

This concept of relaxing eyes with palming was preached by ophthalmologist W.H. Bates a century ago. It has been strongly backed as a way of improving eyesight by Dr. Christiane Northrup, known for her methods of healing all parts of the body, and it has been denounced by others as nonsense. Whether or not it does reduce my need for glasses, I find this can reduce eye strain and make things clearer after I do it for few moments.

Palming is a simple process of covering closed eyes with the palms but not putting pressure on the eyeballs. The fingers should be crossed, right over left or vice versa, on the forehead with the palms over the closed eyes. The ideal is total darkness so arrange the hands to achieve this. The original idea is that palming can relax muscles, and darkness can soothe the optic nerve.

Today, it is recommended as a way to reduce the blue light of steady computer use. Every hour, one should pause and palm for five minutes to practice looking at something long distance. When I first tried this, I visualized seeing Mt. Hood, some 40 miles from my Oregon bedroom window when I was age 12. Another vision came to me of myself floating down the Sandy River in an inner tube with my dad. All kinds of fun memories have floated in my mind's eye.

Palming now is a method for me to make positive intentions that form part of my prayer life. Whether or not it will reduce my need for glasses is not my purpose, but it certainly does create a calmness in me and a form of clearer vision when I return to the world of sight.

So find a way to prop up your arms on a table or with pillows so you don't have to bend over or be tense with unsupported arms. Perhaps palming will bring you surprises in your sight as it has for me.

Palming

We use our hands to block our sight
to see what's in our mind's eye.
Our hands can minimize our stress
and calm our breathing with a sigh.
A short trip into mind-fulness
can revive us for the day.
We never know what clue will come
to spur us on our way.

Sculpting

We are terrestrial beings, on and of the Earth. The remedy for what ails us may be as near as our backyards. Dig in.
                                    Anne MxGregor Parsons, Mother Earth Living

On my desk is a sculpture of a four-pointed black star with faint red inner painting with tiny shell and cone designs. I'm not sure that my youngest granddaughter who gifted me with it was aware that those four points could connect her with earth, air, water, and fire. I treasure her creation.

Clay is more than a plaything for potters. Before it can be molded, it must be softened with water and ground repeatedly before being shaped and then baked in an oven. It is a creative process to birth an object from dirt.

Potter Marjory Zoet Bankston in her book, *The Soulwork of Clay*, writes of seven steps found in transforming clay into the web that connects potters to elements of earth, air, and water. She finds the sculpting process includes breathing and awakening, staying centered, and playing with the creative decision of how to transform the clay.

Molding clay is a process which connects the maker with earth itself. It helps one to center in one's own body the ability to bring life to one's soul. And this gives rise to the spiritual process of wholeness.

People have lost touch with the Earth.
From a biblical perspective, people who
lose touch with the Earth lose touch with God.

Gabriel Cousens, MD, Spiritual Nutrition

Sculpting

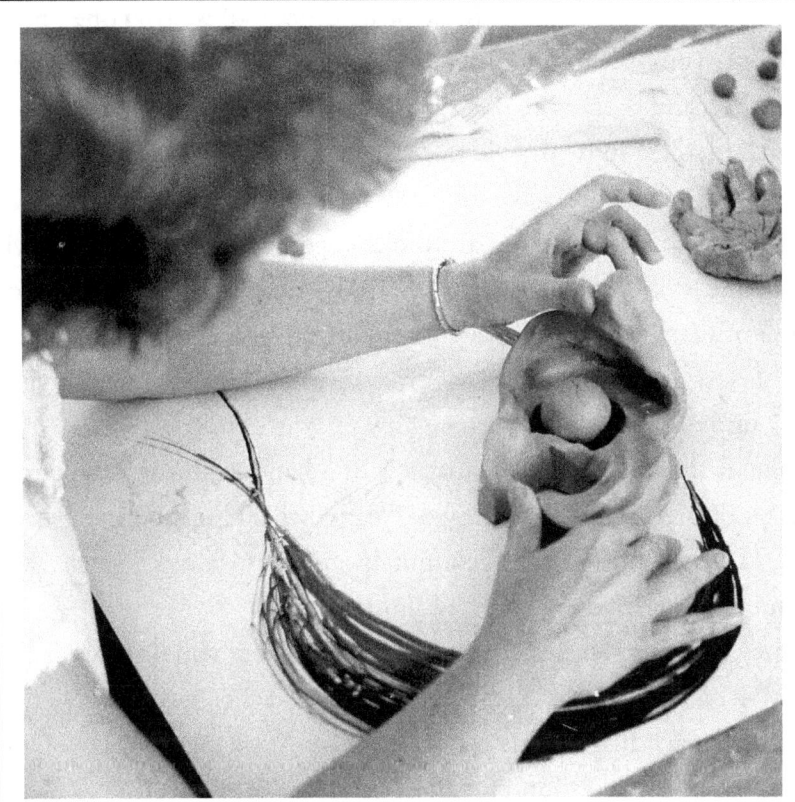

Soul of sand, ground of grime
clinging clay, dust adrift
out of the earth you formed us
arms and legs
rolled and shaped
ears and eyes
molded and smoothed
fannies and thighs
patted and plumped
Creator,
did you have fun playing in the sand?

Cavewriting

Cavewriting is one of nine tools that Barry Lane, author of *Writing as a Road to Self-Discovery*, suggests to help the process of writing one's memories on paper. As young children often do, they put a drawing of a person or object on paper, and then write some single words about the subject. The writer can then add a few more drawings or words and look at it often.

My 13th grandchild gave me such a drawing when she was perhaps 10. It has seven gold stars dancing around a large white quarter moon with the stamp of the world in the distance. It is labeled SPACE. This is from the youngest of six children who shared a small bedroom with big twin beds and a small closet with a sister. Was it her memory of hoping for more space while growing up?

One of the oldest cave paintings is of a hand found in a cave in Spain, maybe 64,000 years old made by a Neanderthal, long believed not to be human. Hands, along with large animals and some constellations, were frequent subjects for cave drawings by humans.

Barry Lane also suggests Hand Mapping where you draw your hand on paper. Write a feeling you have in each finger and then write experiences that connect with each finger. This can be done with spiritual aspects of your life as well. A simple meditation prayer!

> *Something miraculous happens when you write.*
> *It is a way of discovering truth in memory, and with*
> *that discovery comes new knowledge and insight.*

Barry Lane

Cavewriting

I'm drawing like a child with memories of my past
much like our early ancestors who drew their art to last.
They etched and cut their signs on walls in caves
drawings that are here today much to historic raves.

I etch my world on paper of the lights that I can see
stars and planets in the sky where I often hoped to flee.
It's how I spent my summers dreaming of a world up high
leaving cave-like symbols to make my descendants sigh.

Playing

Sister Jose Hobday, a Native American spiritual writer, has shared: "I love to play with God as if I were a child playing with my parents. I like going to the playground, getting in a swing, and swinging high, because I believe God lives in us through the joy and power we sense when we swing high."

I once sponsored a spiritual program for 50 women led by Sister Jose. I forget the topic but I remember taking a tray of strawberries to share. She wanted to see the berries before agreeing to use them. Once she saw them still with stems, she accepted them. Native Americans believe the stem preserves the freshness of the fruit. She also mentioned they would be sweet because the tiny seeds were black, not still green.

I never knew strawberries had a spiritual purpose, since I had spent three summers in junior high picking strawberries in Oregon fields and having to stem them. That was no play but hard work now done by migrant workers. One day I earned a low 50 cents; one summer I earned $40 for the whole season to buy fall school clothes.

We don't need bats and balls or nets and fancy uniforms to play. Abilities don't count and skills are minor. Toddlers walking in a park stop to play with the gold leaves of the Dandelion in the grass. Children hang from bars of playground equipment, and elders play solitaire with cards or guessing games with each other. Sculpting and drawing are creative forms of spiritual play.

> ***It is a happy talent to know how to play.***
> ***When Hindus speak of the creation of the universe,***
> ***they don't call it the work of God.***
> ***They call it the play of God.***

Ralph Waldo Emerson

Playing

Hanging high to hold me
reaching low to feel free
No longer do we sit and dig
in dirt below a school yard tree.
A recess time from classes
A break from learning stats
A jungle gym tests arms and legs
and feeds the brain at that!

Swimming

Faith liberates but fear paralyzes is one saying that can be applied to learning the art of swimming.

Babies seem to love going in water, while older toddlers, who have been taught a bit about the fearful danger of traffic and deep water, are often quite hesitant.

But the benefits of learning to use arms and legs in the art of swimming include greater muscle strength, better breathing, and ability to save one's own life when a boat overturns.

You can flap your arms like a butterfly or paddle like a puppy for many benefits. Research from Australia studied children who frequently swam were able to learn languages easier, develop motor skills, and gain confidence sooner than non-swimmers.

Swimmers often feel an emotional and physical high when natural endorphins activate. As in yoga, swimmers often experience a similar feeling of relaxation. On the spiritual level this is often compared to the practice of mindfulness with swimming being a "moving meditation."

The repetition of the body in constant motion combines with a deep breathing rhythm that offers swimmers a unique form of relaxation. The simple experience alone of floating offers calmness and peace on a level well beyond the often frantic pace of daily living.

Swimming

One hand guides and one gives a push
The swim coach starts to teach
my childish arms to learn to swim
like noble fish who have a fin.

The water ripples oh so gently
but my fear still fills my heart
to paddle bravely in the pool
will make me feel really cool.

Feeding

The hand in our photo could be holding an apple or herbs for the rhinoceros lucky enough to reside in an animal park. Although greyish brown in color, it is a white rhino with large round soft lips for its diet of herbs with teeth farther back in the mouth so its ability to bite the human hand is minimal. The rhino is one of the oldest and largest land mammals with fewer than 30,000 left in their native Africa and Asia. It can stand up to 7 feet high and 13 feet long and weigh from three to five tons.

Most rhinos are solitary animals who usually avoid each other, but the white rhino can live in groups of up to ten. They have poor eyesight but very acute hearing and are agile enough to run up to 45 miles per hour. Their greatest occupation is to roll and play in mud.

One or two horns are their prize possessions, and it is humans who are their enemies. The horn, made of keratin like hair and nails, has no healing value, although poachers kill the animals for the horn previously used in ceremonies or medical medicines. A horn can be removed and will regrow if the skull is not damaged.

About 3,300 rhinos are alive today in natural habitats. The San Diego Zoo has been working to conserve them since 1952.

Help for rhinos: San Diego Zoo Global has done a great deal of conservation work with rhinos, especially once San Diego Zoo Safari Park opened in the 1970s. It has the most successful captive breeding program for rhinoceroses in the world. By July 2019, there had been a total of 184 rhino births at the Safari Park since it opened. animals@sandiegozoo.org

So what, I wonder, did the Creator plan when fashioning a rhino? Someone to help with landscaping by keeping jungle forest floors tidy? Some creature to relish rolling in the mud?

Feeding

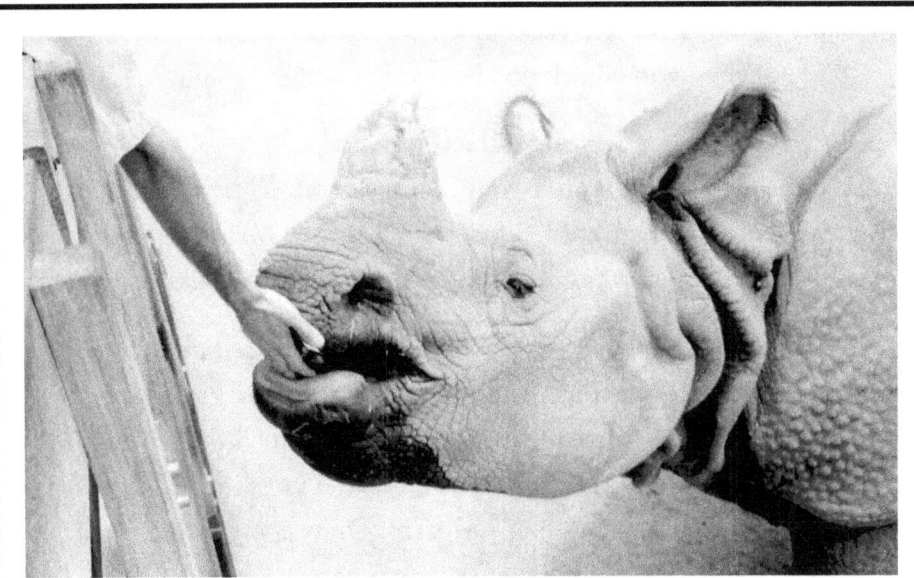

Precious as my hand is
I trust it to a rhino
Feeling its lips so soft and round
that pulls its food from off the ground.
It roams a park where it is safe
its horn a well-sought prize.
I hope it finds my gentle touch
a bit of love it needs so much.

Meditation: Blessed Earth

In the beginning, God created the heavens and earth . . . Gen1

Hold a plant or go outside and stand barefoot on grass or dirt.

Touch the soil . . .
Imagine the Divine breath of the dirt. Watch a bit of Earth form into a human being. Feel yourself emerging from the earth and living in your body. Know that you are good!

Feel yourself growing
like the plant before you or grass beneath your feet. Stretch up to breathe deeply of air needed for life. Push your roots deep in dirt. Reach out your arms and let them flutter in the air like leaves.
Know that growth is good.

Stand tall, placing your feet securely on the ground.
Inhale and exhale, sending down in the earth all the tension and disharmony you feel. As you breathe in, fill your lungs with air, soak up strength of the earth. Draw energy from earth.
Know that energy is good.

Creator
Help us take off the heavy shoes that keep us
from contact with the life of our Mother Earth.
Help us as we struggle to revere the sacredness
of dirt and the sanctity of natural food.
We thank you for the energy from Mother Earth, the majestic
mountains, roaring rivers, and towering trees
We know that earth is good!

Blessed Earth

Holy Mother Earth we bare our feet for you
We give you thanks for mountains
trees that give us fruit
We bless the holy waters
pools to fish and swim
We thank the scented flowers
herbs to heal and drink
We open up our hearts and minds
to hug you as our Mother
nourishing us with milk of love
a spiritual treat from high above.

*Let us pray with the most common things around us.
There is nothing more common than dirt!*

Carol Bialock RSCJ

Foot History

Scientific America writes to explain the rather complicated and not well-known history of human feet. It is easier to understand by those proficient in Latin the names of foot bones which make up one fourth of the human skeleton. Here is a very simple version for those of us rusty with our Latin.

Humans and chimpanzees are often compared for similar body parts, but samples of the two creatures prove some but not total similarity. Chimps millions of years ago had feet that functioned like four hands with different grasping abilities. Later human discoveries found the tarsal and metatarsal bones that form the plane of the human foot had no toes.

In 1995, scientists suggested the ankle joint and heel (the hindfoot) existed before the anatomy of the human forefoot as it pertains to bipedalism. The human foot evolved independently of other developments within human evolution and at different rates between species. The adaptation of the human foot cannot be explained linearly although even some 3.3 million years ago, it was possible to see it as allowing for the eventually walking on two, rather than four feet. *Scientific American Guy 2015*

Technology has changed the way humans walk! *Scientific America* suggests that while texting on cell phones, humans are less likely to trip because they shorten their step length, reduce step frequency, lengthen the time during which both feet are in contact with the ground, and increase obstacle clearance height. This seems to slow texters so they can be more aware of their surroundings. Awareness is a strong element in becoming authentic.

Foot History

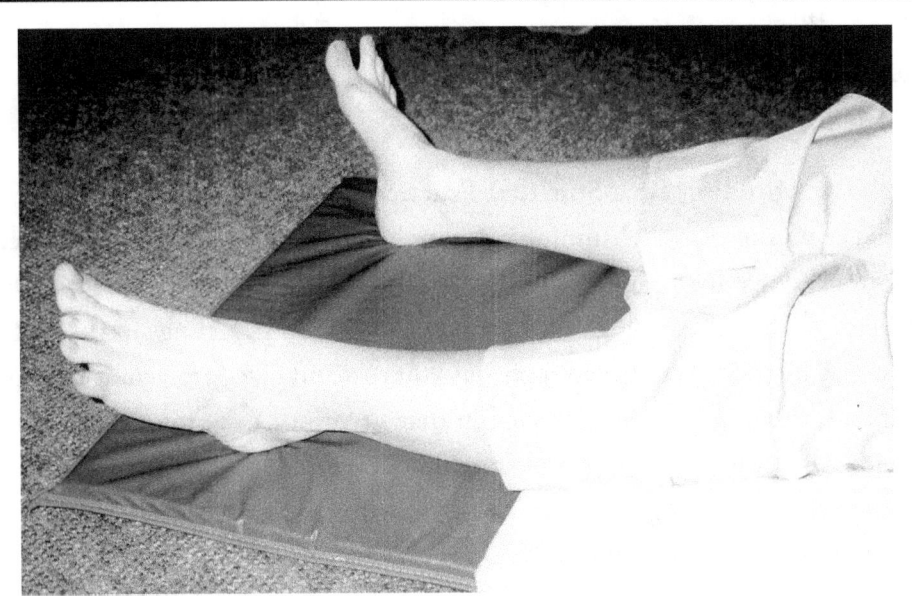

You walk like a farmer. my mother used to say.
You walk like a farmer. Sr. Edward said at school.
You walk like a farmer. I bounced a basketball.
You walk like a farmer. I rode my two-wheel bike.
You walk like a farmer. I danced at Polish weddings.
You walk like a farmer, I chased toddlers in the street.
You walk like a farmer.
I'm glad I have two feet.

Walking/Running

Even the youthful may faint and grow weary,
And youths stagger and fall,
They that hope in the Lord will renew their strength,
they will soar as with eagles' wings
They will run and not grow weary,
walk and not grow faint.
Isaiah 40:30-31

Can Running Be a Spiritual Practice? A website called the *peacefulrunner.com* suggests the running actually helps people become more peaceful in everyday lives. Spirituality is about discovering one's true self in this process . . . about letting go of troubling emotions and feelings in the body.

Pay attention to your thoughts as you run and give forgiveness to yourself and whoever might be involved in that situation. You can replace resentments with peace. This is a simple practice to do while running or walking. If you are in a rural area with trees and dirt paths, you can drink in the nature surrounding you.

If you run in city blocks, give unhealthy memories to the clouds and stars above. Runners often get 'a high' and envision that as riding on the clouds of authenticity, joy, and peace. Wherever your imagination goes, your spirit goes, believes the peacefulrunner.com.

> *Running doubles as a spiritual experience featuring many aspects of prayer—a chance to quiet the mind, test personal limits, and suffer on behalf of a mission. I often pray while I'm running because of that very peaceful experience of the very fluid moving of your body . . .*
>
> Sr. Stephanie Baliga, Franciscan, runner in 8 marathons

Walking/Running

My legs are long I value them
while I'm on the inside track.
I can run free from all my care
as wind blows through my hair.
My Spirit floats so fast before me
I'm out to catch that special essence
that makes me more than merely mortal
as I rise spiritually on this human portal.

Stretching

Stretching is controversial! You might need to approach stretching with caution. If you have a chronic condition/injury, you might need to adjust your stretching techniques. For example, if you already have a strained muscle, stretching it may cause further harm.

Mayo Clinic Staff

The Mayo Clinic has long lists of how to stretch safely, and it generally approves of the process. Harvard and *Sports Medicine* websites praise this effort to stretch muscles and gain flexibility, while the *British Journal of Sports Medicine* claims there is no evidence that stretching prevents injuries.

Several years ago on Christmas Eve as I was blowing many leaves from our side yard, I tripped backwards and fell against our wooden fence, directly on my back ribs. Three chiropractors find no damage, but whenever I walk for more than ten minutes, I get a heavy pressure in my back ribs. When I lay flat and stretch my arms high above my head, the pressure leaves.

I suspect my aging skeleton is slumping and a long stretch relieves the pressure so I often stop to gently stretch during my daily walk.

So be aware that stretching has its limits, but benefits do improve a range of motion of physical abilities and better blood flow. Stress can lessen and calmness can move the body into a level of relaxation that helps body and soul join together. These are certainly worth the effort.

We only need to move through a healthy range of motion . . . beyond that we can strain muscles and tendons and compromise joint health.

Sage Roundtree, *Institute Journal of Sports Physical Therapy*

Stretching

I reach the ground and touch the sky
when stretching hands and feet
I am a connector between the two
while on my earthly beat.
I'm here on earth like humans all
yet act like angels from above
spreading blessings to one and all
gifting them with spiritual love.

Dancing

"Dance is imagination brought to life! Dance is prayer. Dance is meditation. Dance is walking through the clouds, flying among the stars, gliding on the moon, and experiencing the pure bliss of heaven on earth."
La'Toya Princess Jackson 2016

"Dance is the fastest, most direct route to the truth -- not some big truth that belongs to everybody, but the personal kind, the what's-happening-in-me-right-now kind of truth. We dance to reclaim our brilliant ability to disappear in something bigger, something safe, a space without a critic or a judge or an analyst."
Gabrielle Roth, Spiritual Power of Dance 2012

"Praise dancing is a liturgical or spiritual dance that incorporates music and movement as a form of worship rather than as an expression of art or as entertainment. Praise dancers use their bodies to express the word and spirit of God. Rather than tights . . . praise dancers wear loose-fitting, modest attire, aimed at keeping the audience's attention on the spirituality they're trying to convey, rather than the bodies being used to convey it."
Treva Bedinghaus Liturgical Dance as a Form of Worship 2019

"Sufi whirling," is dervish dancing— a form of moving meditation channeled into a spinning dance. As we know, all of life follows a circular pattern: our blood, menstrual cycles, seasonal cycles, planetary cycles. By aligning with the natural pattern inherent in existence, dervish dances also merge with the divine, by entering altered states of consciousness with bliss and pure being."
Althea Luna, 5 Types of Spiritual Dancing That Connect w/Eternity

Dancing

Spirit move in us. Spirit breathe in us. We are one in you.
Song words guide our dancing feet
Billowing a flowing haze
gently keeping time to heartthrobs
as we float in soulful praise.
Spirit dance in us. Spirit sing in us. We are song in you.
Song rhythm lifts our singing souls
Filling out our church as stage
Moving voice with feet of joy
With Spirit great we do engage.
Spirit we are free in you. We are whole in you
We are one in you.
Song lyrics from **Spirit Move In Us, Hello, Life!**
A Woman's Journey *by Bonnie Randolph Gibson*

Orchestra of Feet

The First Time

From the floor I watched the legs above me
walk and run and kneel and so I learned to walk.
My first steps shaky, wobbly, my heart throbbing
but I stood strong, determined to move on my own.
On my bike I watched the riders around me
push and pedal and brake and so I learned to ride.
My first try was jerky, slow, my heart was pumping
but I kept on, determine to master my bike.
In a basketball game, I watched players dribble
bouncing the ball so I jerked right and left,
Toes tipping, knees flipping, my heart was a pounding,
but I shot baskets and scored high in my life.

Right I Walk

I start my walk by turning right, my feet are nimbly clad.
I watch the sidewalk carefully to fall would be so bad.
A mile I walk just turning right each time I end a block.
It brings me to Las Palmas park where summer ducks do dock.
I watch the tennis balls go whiz as round those courts I go.
Right past the dog park on the left up hilly lawns I slow.
Another right where children play past baseball in the field.
I finally make a left turn home with exercise my yield.
Today I shall reverse my walk, turning left is what I'll do
to see the world a different way and exercise my brain anew.

Orchestra of Feet

On cue. The orchestra tunes
Soles fan the air like birds on a wing.
On cue. The melody rises
Soles keep the rhythm like fish in a school.
On cue. The tempo slows
Each sole reaches up bare-ing its soul!

***Sisters, It is much easier to reach for the stars
when your feet are on the ground.***

Elizabeth Mangham

Boots

Walking ahead to meet the Lord with bare feet – the Sikhs, the Hindus, the Jains, the Buddhists – they all do that in our part of the world.
Dr. Cajetan Coelho

The Christian Bible has many references to feet and shoes, particularly in reference to spiritual warfare and need for a strong foothold. Early Christians needed to wear combat boots to stand up and fight against the devil and other forms of evil. They provided the wearer with mobility and endurance. Boots and sandals were necessary to wear on a path to peace!

Marina McCoy, an associate professor at Boston College, tells her story of wearing boots in Spain on a pilgrimage. Carefully, she selected and practiced wearing the boots before her long walk, but still she developed blisters. Day after day blisters plagued her, so she stopped to buy a pair of sandals which she alternated in wearing on her hike.

Finally, one day she stopped and removed her boots from her backpack and left them behind. It added to her spiritual journey because she also mentally left unwanted things in her life behind her. She just tossed them away as she moved into a freer life.

Happiness consists in finding out precisely what "the one thing necessary" may be in our lives, and in gladly relinquishing all the rest. For then, by a divine paradox, we find that everything else is given us together with the one thing we needed.
Thomas Merton, No Man Is an Island

Just how important are our fancy boots and stiletto heels as bare necessities in life? Boots can be bought on websites with spiritual names like *Peace and Love, Enlightenment, Spiritual Butterflies and LiveLoveLaugh.*
yeswevibe.com

Boots

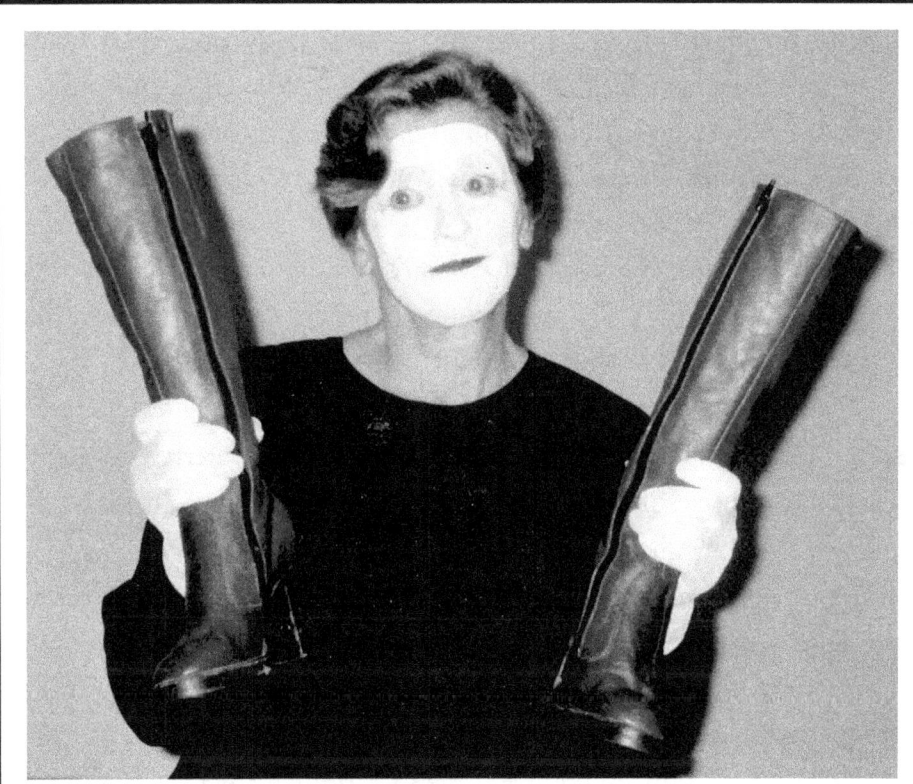

These boots were made for walking
and my white face for disguise.
The heels are high but still quite sturdy
for my comic act so wise.
I know it's only cause I'm acting
that my white gloves match my face,
but it helps me please the audience
just want to set a laughing pace.

Shoes

Jewish teachings in the 17th century write of the need for "spiritual shoes as a shield between a person and the earth. Those who walked barefoot were shunned by God."

The Christian bible tells the story of Moses at the burning bush who was told by God to remove his shoes because he was "standing on holy ground."

In the early days of Rome, citizens had the right to wear sandals. Feet symbolized an inner state and to go barefoot suggested a spiritual poverty. By the Middle Ages, pilgrims would walk barefoot as penance for their sins or as a sign of mourning. Going barefoot was common in many biblical texts as respect for holy ground. It is a common act today for folk to remove shoes upon entering holy places.

There is no one pair of shoes that marks the beginning of shoemaking because different cultures and locations used different materials. Shoes have been found on cave drawings some 40,000 years ago. In cold areas, thick leather was used, while palm leaves met the need in southern regions.

Egyptians sandals and pointed shoes were worn in the 12th century, when heels were added to shoes. At that time one's social class determined the type and style of shoe. In the Middle Ages seaports in Europe were centers for craftsmen in designing useful and fashionable shoes.

Shoes today know no bounds in styles with high stiletto heels and diamond studded flip-flops. The Earthing movement teaches us that going barefoot 15 minutes a day allows feet to absorb healing powers from the earth, but wearing synthetic shoes or going barefoot on fake turf made from old rubber tires is not a spiritual choice.

> ***Of all the paths you take in life***
> ***make sure a few of them are dirt.***
>
> Wild Woman Sisterhood

Shoes

In barefoot lands where feet run free
no laces found to tie them down
where skin gets tough on pebbly path
bare feet don't get a frown.
Two dozen pairs of shoes line up
saving feet from cuts and bruises
loafer, sandal, tennis shoe
they all are not one but two.
Some shield our skin from rocky roads
synthetic shoes ban heathy soil
there is time and place to make a choice
shoes do affect our spiritual toil!

IV Pray-ers

Prayer is a communication with a spiritual being. Spiritual prayer can be saying words, making music, creating art, lighting candles or incense. God can be the sun, moon, earth, a feminine figure, a male crusader, or an invisible energy called God, Creator, Yahweh, Buddha, or more. Most any expression we make, object we use, or person we talk to can fit the definition of the process of prayer.

Prayers answer many needs of humans. Adoration, asking favors, giving thanks, and confessing sins are common reasons. For hundreds of centuries, prayer has been associated with healing.

The 'energy' movement in recent years has brought into use a new form of prayer – positive thoughts done by groups or individuals who want to heal. Lynne McTaggart, author of eight books and a spiritual leader in the world, wrote **The Intention Experiment** which describes scientific experiments resulting from group positive thought.

This is not to downplay or replace the formal prayers used by various religions. They have caused many miracles, but as we learn about energy and our role in healing, we can form specific words for specific results, and positive scientific results have been documented.

My daily prayers now include positive thoughts that I want to become reality. Since I have a serious eye condition, I have asked family members to pray daily: "Mom's eyes can see clearly and read newsprint. Her eyes are normal, and healthy." I say nothing negative but just a statement of how I want the situation to be in present tense.

For 50 years, I have used prayer and natural remedies to heal and develop a great relationship with angels and the Divine.

Someone is listening!

Meditation: Connect with Soul

This can help clear your mind and increase concentration during meditation or any time that requires concentration.
Incense can help reduce stress and restore emotional balance.
It also enhances psychic abilities and induces sleep.

*Please find a comfortable seat, relax,
sit with your hands open. Close your eyes.*
Imagine your body circled by a cloud of light…a healing light that is always around and inside of you—the light of your Creator.
Just rest, breathe in, and feel the comfort of the light.

See light on all sides of you. . . left - right - behind - in front of you. Now see and feel the light side of you in every cell of your body connecting you to the Divine. Believe this is a form of prayer that washes and renews your body and comes from the Divine Source.
Believe this is renewing your body.

You may feel warmth, some tingling, or a sensation of energy.
As you open to our Creator, you can feel the healing essence
of divinity that flows into every part of your life.
Perhaps your light has an energizing color - gold, purple, blue.
Rest and breathe in the color. See it coming from above.

Envision the light coming into your head bringing love and hope.
See it as a river of light flowing through your heart connecting with love and compassion. Allow it to flow below your waist for creativity.
You are a bridge of light from heaven to earth, connecting the Divine.

**Place your hands on your heart in prayer and gratitude.
You are a fountain of light filled with the Light of all.**

Holy Mother

Mother's Day comes but once a year
but you are precious every day
We've called you he and man so much
we want to pray in this new way
We raise our arms in praise of you
giving thanks for food and water
blessing air and warmth of fire
We are both son and daughter.
We know that you are gender-free
beyond all time and space
You can always hear our praise for you
and you know us each by our face.

Candles

When I was growing up, taking part in a 9-day Novena for a spiritual reason was common practice. It is one I used often in my college days and one I rely on today in this troubled world to get heavenly attention for a cause. My college intention was personal but had unbelievable success.

Lighting a small candle is key in my process. Today when someone needs a job or a grandchild is in a car accident, I light a small candle for nine days. It goes in an Owl holder which has a place to put lavender drops on the top. I believe my request is not just heaven-sent but earthly-scent.

The history of candle making began with the discovery of fire almost 800,000 years ago. The earliest users likely were the Ancient Egyptians, who made torches by soaking the pithy core of reeds in melted animal fat. However, it had no wick. Beeswax, which burned cleanly without a smoky flame, replaced animal fat in the Middle Ages.

The light of candles dates to the time God was thought to be light from the sun. Theology considered it a Divine Light, an aspect of the presence of a divinity. It meant light in a time of darkness. Colored candles carry individual meanings that match with colors of chakra energy: red is for physical grounding; orange is creativity; yellow is emotion, sky blue for communication; and green is the heart and love. Energy centers above the heart are purple and white.

Some believe that color has the same energy as that organ it represents in the human body. Black is a color without energy while a white candle meets all needs. Candles can adapt to make light for any reason when our world gets dim.

Candles

Each hand is like the candle
holding light within its power
brightening up the world
like a newly blossomed flower.
The flame catches our eyes
and brings hope to dark insides.
The sacred warmth fills us
and makes us want to sing:

***It only takes a spark
to get a fire going
that's how it is with God's love.***

From Pass it On

Meditation: Holy Fire

Find a favorite place in a darkened room. Light a candle.
Play meditative music if you wish. Breathe deeply and relax.

Focus on the dark.
In your mind, visualize you are in outer space in the darkened earth before the sun was made. There are no stars. Imagine total darkness.

Open your eyes
Focus on the candle light. See how it reveals the outline of the candle. The flame illuminates the air above it. You can see shadows behind it.

Hold the candle in your hand.
Breathe gently around the flittering wick.
Can you hear its silence? Do you smell its wax?

Breathe a gentle breath
Slowly, very slowly inhale and see the flame tilt toward you.
Imagine this light going into your body. Feel the warmth near you.

Imagine the light going in you.
Visualize the flame reaching into your nostrils and into your brain.
It illuminates seeing through your eyes and hearing in your ears.

Feel lightness in your head.
Imagine the flame sliding down your backbone, giving warmth
to your lungs and piercing your heart with lightness and love.
Your creative center perks up. The root center of your body is aglow.

Prayer:
Oh, holy flame of energy, filling my body, you renew every
cell and muscle, every drop of blood and thought process. You fill
my soul with the fire of spiritual energy, with a spark of the Divine.
I am aglow with your Presence.

The most powerful weapon on earth is the human soul on fire.
                                                    Ferdinand Foch

Incense

My bowl of incense I raise high
as whiffs of fragrance lead the way.
We're going to start our daily prayer
just like Wise Men did one day.
Inhale. Inhale. Raise it high.
Its fragrance gives a holy smell.
It is a gift for the Divine and a treat for us as well.

Frankincense was one of the most spiritual spices used for blessings, purification, and safety centuries before Wise Men made it popular. It was used for medical, cultural, and religious reasons. As the smoke rises from burning incense, it is considered to go heavenward. Just as it can clear one's mind and spirit, it can clear negativity from a room.

Music

Music is a moral law. It gives soul to the universe, wings to the mind, flight to the imagination, and charm and gaiety to life and to everything.
                                                                Plato

Our very first experience of music is when we hear our mother's heartbeat as we nestle in her womb. Soon our own heart beats before we venture forth into a world of sound.

Music is what connects us to our divine center . . . our essence and that which takes us to other realms of elevated experiences. It matters little the words or the type . . . sacred songs, country ballads, Irish melodies . . . each type can enrich the human spirit as long as its words are positive, and the singing voices do not shout or yell.

In the 3rd century BC a Greek engineer, Clesibius of Alexandria, devised an instrument called the hydraulic, the forerunner of the organ. By 900 the organ appeared in use in ceremonial purposes; and by 1400, organs known as 'King of all instruments' were well established in European churches.

The piano was invented in 1700 by Italian Bartolomeo Cristofori, a harpsichord maker, who wanted better control of an instrument. He is credited for switching out the plucking mechanism with a hammer to create the modern piano. The name Piano is shortened from pianoforte . . . meaning soft-loud sound. The piano's 88 keys are indeed prayer ways into human adventures by making spirituality a trip into the Divine.

Color is the keyboard, the eyes are the harmonies, the soul is the piano with many strings. The artist is the hand that plays, touching one key or another, to cause vibrations in the soul."
                                                                Wassily Kandinsky

Music

A is for the ache in my Achilles
B is for the burps that burn my throat
C can lower my cholesterol while
D can ease my tummy's bloat
E is for the earache that afflicts me
F can sooth my constant fears
G means ginkgo for my memory lapse
A—sweet A— just hums away my tears.
Put them all together they spell healing
Chords of vitamins to solve my pain
The power of these keys for my wellbeing
scores extra high for spiritual gain.

Statues

When sweet and bitter mingled together, no reed was plaited, no rules muddled the waters. The gods were nameless, careless, futureless.
The History of God, Karen Armstrong

In the very beginning, the idea of a God had no vision. It was unseen . . . an invisible power in outer space, deep in the earth, warm in the sun.

Three visions of a Divine Creator emerged from the primal wasteland. Apsu was identified from sweet water of the rivers, his wife Tamat from the salty sea, and Mummu from the Womb of Chaos. Their names meant abyss, void, or bottomless gulf. They did not have a clear identity.

Other gods emerged, one from another, often in pairs. Myths developed. Finally, one called Marduk created humanity. So ideas of what a God looked like appeared. Karen Armstrong, former Catholic nun, student at Oxford, and literature prof, now foremost British religious commentator, writes in her ninth book, **The History of God**, that all religions are created by humans.

So humans create objects to visualize a divine power. Statues, medals, books, and ceremonies abound in a search for something spiritual. People, with or without religious beliefs, create physical objects to assist them on their path of spirituality to become authentically developed and understand creation.

A mother and baby statue encourages all moms to love regardless of an associated religion. Flowers and fruit from Mother Earth inspire us to value and respect the soil below. Candles, incense, music, and dance all boost thoughts of connecting with some Power we do not see. A crystal stone may replace a medal, a statue made by one's own hands can indeed be an honest vision of what we all seek to understand.

Statues

Two women with their babes in arms
have always been the chosen charms
on my altar of childhood femininity.
But as I grew in wisdom, I learned
of independent Artemis, and wise Athena
Isis with her life and Venus full of beauty.
A rotund Russian doll joined my altar gals
as did others from my hubby's trips afar.
How much of God is she I wondered.
As each of us designs our God
I find these two babes are sweet boys
to balance my gender-sided joys.

Rocks

Belief in the supernatural healing power of rocks existed long before history was written. Early cultures had beliefs in stones and minerals often used for medical uses and spiritual practices. Carl Jung called stones "primordial symbols of eternity."

Rocks are certainly little chunks of history since they have rested in their riverbeds for possibly millions of years. Many religions found various uses for stones. Ancient Mayans and residents of islands in the Pacific used stones as currency. Chinese believed they were a symbol of longevity because they are alive with an energy that does not change over time. Rock gardens for Japanese are an invitation to meditate - a passage into a state of Zen for absorption.

In Christianity Christ and the church are associated with rocks: *The Lord is my rock and my fortress, my strength . . . my shield.* Peter's name in Greek means 'rock,' and that is where Christ built his church.

Avia Venefica, *Digging for Meaning of Stones*

Meditation on a rock

Find a small rock, sit comfortably and hold it in your hand.
Close your eyes, moving back in time to when the rock was created.
Feel the smoothness of the rock giving you calmness.
Touch a jagged point as a gentle prod from century to century.
Think of the gravity of the rock in relation to your connection to earth.
Feel grounded and comfortable with the stone you hold.
Be grateful for the energy of the rock's long life
Be still - and return to life feeling patience and peace.

Rocks

Shells and rocks make a world round
for our retreat at the sandy shore.
We form an altar with earthy treasures
and light a candle for something more.
Seashells hum their echo chamber
starfish add a smile or two.
We each have a special prayer
Holy One . . . we're talking to you.

An Altar/Shrine

A shrine is a powerful expression of spirituality. It is a sacred space that most all spirituality paths in the world have created to better understand a divinity. It is a sign that something deep within ourselves is occurring. It is something to engage our mind, body, and soul as we travel on our path.

Famous shrines exist around the world where people go to pray and ask for miracles, but we can create an altar/shrine for our own daily life. Choose a place in your home . . . a table or bookcase you can cover with a beautiful cloth or doily.

If your altar focuses on one person, place a photo there or a statue. You can surround your object with flowers, candles, stones or seashells, singing bowls, and things of nature. You're creating something that can keep you present in a holy place when you pass it.

You can create a daily ceremony to build up spiritual energy for your thoughts and positive intentions. Spend some time each day at your altar in prayer and meditation. Freshen your flowers or light a small vigil light. Have a notepad to write prayers and hopes each day. Keep some reading material, chimes, or small drums to add a rhythm for your thoughts. Sing yourself a little song or play soft music.

This object will fill your altar with spiritual energy. For many years my office at home was also a room where I held Drumming for Health sessions and spiritual discussion groups. The walls have banners of chakra colors, gorgeous hula hoop-size replicas of a pregnant woman on Earth and a woman pouring Water at the Well.

Those who came meditated, prayed, sang, and drummed for healing and peace on earth. My office where I write is a shrine that fills the whole room with books of many forms of spirituality.

You too can make such a space.

An Altar/Shrine

I light the candle tall and white
to bring some energy my way.
The mallet chimes the singing bowl
teasing its rim to echo this day.
Three holy women connect to pray
to meditate for worldly love
and books are ready to give a quote
casting forth the calmness of dove.
A simple altar. a prayerful shrine
for all the world family, not just mine.

Meditation: Holy Water

Find a favorite place to sit. Fill a glass or bowl with water.
Play meditative music if you wish. Breathe deeply and relax.

Focus on the water.
Imagine yourself floating gently in your mother's womb,
keeping time with the rhythm of her heartbeat.
Visualize your birth, sliding out into the world
with the gush of nourishing pregnant waters.
Our Creator gives us water, and we know that it is good.
Touch the water.
Imagine the trickle of water at your first bath
scantily running off your forehead.
Our Creator washes us with water, and we feel that it is good.
Taste the water.
Feel the coolness of water in your throat as your swallow it.
Savor the sweetness of spiritual water in dry times of life.
Our Creator gives us living water to drink, we taste that it is good.

Prayer: *Nurturing Creator,*
you cradled us in your womb of your spiritual body.
Let me nurse from the breast of your abundance.
Comforting Creator,
you showered us with springs and lakes to quench our thirsts.
Let me drink deeply form the fountain of your love.
Healing Creator,
you lead us through sickness and pain to the
refreshing streams of living water.
Let me inhale energy from the oasis of your peace.
Loving Creator,
you carry the jug of precious, life-sustaining liquid.
Let me sip your living water . . . as I travel 'On My Way'.

Holy Water

Out of the depths we pour ourselves
into the bowl of life
still like the water in a deep dark well
restless like rapids in a roaring river
sharp like the hailstones on a window pane
smooth like a surface of a frozen lake.
Our of our depths our emotions flow
catch them if you can
swirling, dancing, laughing, loving
catch them if you can.

Clowning

. . . let women keep silent in the churches, for it is not permitted for them to speak, but let them be submissive, as the Law also says . . .
1Cor5:34

When I was a small girl some 70 years ago, women were not allowed on the altar of my church except to clean it. Five major religions in the world were male-dominated, and few allowed women to be ordained or have leadership roles.

But at the age of 10 in the fifth grade, I won a reading contest to read a prayer during a May celebration in church. In the contest, I was determined to read really loud. Skinny and shy, I threw my voice to the rafters and won the contest. So in a church where women could not read from the altar, I stood in the congregation and read very loud.

So during the 1990s when I ran a non-profit organization on women's spirituality, I organized five women's gatherings where up to some 500 women raised their voices in song and readings . . . more often in high school gyms than in churches.

Spirit on the Way

Women the Way is a phrase that we have chosen
walking on a path sometimes icy, often frozen
Slipping on a story that has only males in it
Feminists will say, "it's time to take and end it."
We need our rites and symbols to be fully whole
to balance how we pray is our simple goal.
We want female to be of an equal measure
Spirituality with both is what we want to treasure.
At this time we ask women to act and think anew
Flipflop images of God and make them gender-few.
Can we image God as tree or maybe woman on a cross
Masculine-only images are what we want to toss.

Clowning

Hey, Sophia God . . .
We're clowning around
laughing in your place
our place . . . altar space . . . your space
putting on the white face
singing what we feel inside
shouting out our joy
cheering like a noisy mob
lifting hands on high
chanting . . . swaying . . . celebrating
holding hands and syncopating.
Do you really want us to be quiet here?

Stringing Along

Awake, Arise women of life
Awake, Arise women of joy
Awake, Arise women of honor
Awake, Arise women of heart
Awake, Arise women of light
. . . women of hope and love and one voice.

On June 24, 1994, some 500 women and a few men gathered in a Silicon Valley high school gym to celebrate a day-long gathering called "Women Awakening."

The women celebrated the awakening of the feminine in their spiritual beliefs in a ceremony as they danced and sang Four Dreams.

1. Power of Birthing and Creativity
2. Power of Intuition
3. Power of Feelings
4. Power of the Body

The Awakening: Dreams during slumber often bring insight and growth. The women celebrated with song and dance.

Women join hands, sing with one voice.
We are a light, we are a sign.
Women join hands, sing with one voice.
"We are the hope of our time."

Song words/music by Bonnie Randolph Gibson

Stringing Along

Women in a gym oh what are they doing
Not tossing balls in hoops
so what are they playing?
Are they stringing us along
in a strange new way of praying?
There is someone in the center
leading all the gals in song
are they doing something right
or have they got the gym all wrong?

***We are women giving birth to life
we are women giving birth to life!***
Lyrics by Bonnie Randolph Gibson

Labyrinth

Set your feet to the path for there is no other way.

A Magic Dwells, Joan Marie McMillen

A labyrinth is an ancient symbol representing wholeness. It uses the imagery of the circle in a wandering path for a journey into one's own center and back again out into the world. It is a tool of meditation. This is the labyrinth in the Chartres Cathedral in France built in the 12th century. You can start at the bottom and trace your way into the center as you are going into your own center. Pause to meditate before repeating your steps on the way out.

Labyrinth

Shoulder to shoulder we pull our tape
across the muddied swirls of marble
side by side our paths lead us beyond
in space unseen . . . in time unknown
together yet alone.
Spirituality a journey we follow outside ourselves
to find ourselves . . . inside ourselves
Watch out Creator . . . here we come!

Labyrinth in photo being laid on a gym floor.

This is the place where the longed-for will happen
This is the time where the longed-for will come . . .

Remembering the Way, Joan Marie McMillen

Body, Mind, Soul

I am body
The vessel of your senses . . . an orchestra of organs
A labyrinth of arteries . . . a maze of cells and bones
I am eyes for seeing color . . . ears for hearing sound
Backbone for support . . . feet to walk on ground.
I . . . am . . . body.
Breathing, moving, working . . . hands and feet and brains
A most marvelous creation . . . feeling joy and pain
I am structure for your mind . . . I am shelter for your soul
I am one part of your being . . . but intrinsic to your whole.
I am mind.
A container for your thinking . . . a scrapbook for your memory
The source of your perception . . . a cup for understanding
I can think and I can reason . . . I imagine and create
I hold the past and future . . . yet live within the now.
I . . . am . . . mind!
I am consciousness . . . connected and aware
I direct the show and even star . . . in the story of your life
I am rooted in your body . . . I am woven in your soul
I am one part of your being . . . but intrinsic to your whole.
I am soul.
The essence of your being . . . the breath of the divine
A cradle for emotions . . . a great mystery in life
I am site for meditation . . . a center for your prayer
A harbor in a rainstorm . . . a ticket out of strife.
I . . . am . . . soul!
I encourage you to stop and see . . . the beauty of the sky
The sacredness of nature . . . the nuisance of the fly
I am essence of your body . . . I am master of your mind.
I am one part of your being . . . but intrinsic to your whole.
I . . . am . . . body . . . mind . . . and soul! *Arlene Goetze*

Body, Mind, Soul

*I feel loved
by the touch of a dear skin
on my back.
I draw serenity
from resting my deer skin
on one I love.
May our dear hug calm you as it does us.*

V. Memories

The soul thrives on remembering. Feed it memories and it comes alive.
                        Spiritual writer Macrina Wiederkehr

But take care and watch yourselves closely, so as neither to forget the things that your eyes have seen nor to let them slip from your mind all the days of your life; make them known to your children and your children's children.

                                                            Deuteronomy 4:9

Remember what you have seen, because everything forgotten returns to the circling winds."

                                                             Navajo chant

Photography is one simple way to remember our past so let this section of photos be brief memories worth a smile or an insight! As a journalist since 1956, I carried a camera with me to record events I wrote about.

Only a few of those thousand pictures I took have been published in newspapers and books for viewers to taste and see. Most are memories pasted in photo albums or in boxes in the closet. Most were taken before the days of cell phone cameras.

For Christmas 2018 I went through dozens of boxes of photos of our family . . . sorting photos for some seven children, spouses, and 18 grandchildren . . . and filled each stocking with the photos of their younger years.

According to their responses, it was the greatest gift they received. It is impossible to count the gifts that our Divine Creator has given us, but memories and cameras have to be two of them.

Recording the Spiritual

People often write autobiographies and histories of their lives, but collecting memories of one's spiritual life is less common. One way to have both physical and spiritual memories for later life is to make a box or drawer filled with physical memories of spiritual lives.

Make yourself or someone you love a Spiritual Box to hold booklets, quotes, prayer cards . . . things that can give comfort when memories start to fade. Include the memories of your favorite prayers and ceremonies, add a favorite candle holder, statue, piece of music to comfort yourself, as well as photos of spiritual events. A dried red flower or lavender sachet can add scents of cheer. Photos can indeed reflect one's life in many phases and be great comfort indeed.

Anthony de Mello, Indian Jesuit priest and author of spiritual teachings, suggests the following exercises to have spiritual encounters with God.

**Return to some scene in which you felt deeply loved . . . How was this love shown to you? In words, looks, gestures, an act of service, a letter? Stay with the scene as long as you experience something of the joy that was yours when this event took place.

**Return to some scene in which you felt joy. What produces this joy in you? Good news . . . the fulfillment of some desire . . . a scene of nature? Recapture the original scene and the feelings that accompanied it. Stay as long as you can with these feelings.

You can add symbols of such feelings of love and joy to your Spiritual Box. Acts of such mindfulness can increase one's ability to experience God in both the physical and spiritual worlds.

Recording the Spiritual

Smile! Everybody smile!
Click. Snap.
A moment in the present
recorded for the future
to remember the past.
How can two simple mirrors
reflect one body nine times over
for shooting something minor
at a meeting where folks wear name tags.
Smile. Don't blink!
Your present photo is now past
to remember in the future.

Purrfect Memories

2009

The stars today on my walk so fast
are spirits from my feline past.
Four cats I nurtured and loved with care
eyed me as I passed their lair.
One found his way some twenty feet
to sniff my hand and honor my greet.
His owner shocked he came to me
a past life owner I might be.

A second cat in her driveway sun
absorbed earth's energy, a cat's real fun
but then I saw Caesar locked in a stare
did he remember me from somewhere?
Could I be the one who fed him 20 years
a black and white king among all his peers.
I petted and hugged and gave him his wish
canned food he wanted in his plastic dish.

And last there was Cuddles, that gold neighbor cat
who always was waiting on our side door mat.
She stared as I passed her in her sunny new life
glad to be rid of the old one with strife.
My life is now vacant, not one cat to purr
my stress times away as I pet soft sleek fur.
I still do envision the cats that we had
They're still in my memory and I am so glad!

*2020: Catnip, a young feral cat, now fills
our time, laps, and beds.*

Purrfect Memories

Portia and Paris
Shylock and Caesar
Our cats all bore an elegant name
that speaks of great literature fame.
One copied the toddlers' bathroom skills
He used the kid's potty when empty or filled
and one peeked in windows of folks on our block
like his birth owner of Watergate stock.
On summer vacations wherever we went
one wore wet towels to cool by the car's vent.
Sometimes I forget the power of cats
and how much love they really have meant!

A Son's Spirit

The components of an inborn spirituality are countless. When babies are born, we count the fingers and toes, look in blue or brown eyes, and especially let the baby grasp one of our fingers. Touching another human is one of the first great connectors of love and trust.

The first section of this book focuses on virtues and values that shine forth even in simple photos of innocent children. Parents are overwhelmed at the enormous task they now have to raise a child both physically and spiritually.

Rather than a long list of what-to-do, we can simply live our own spirituality when raising children. Let them copy us as we

- Ask a blessing for food before a meal and give thanks for the presence of sons and daughters companionship and care
- Take long walks in parks or woods, encouraging children to pick up a colored leaf or small stick to talk about
- Urge children to talk to the bees in a lavender bush or crows on a grassy field
- Have the child give a donation to a homeless person while passing one in a parking lot or by a store door
- Stand and admire a rainbow after rain, a full or partial moon, or trees on the side of hills and mountains

Developing a spiritual nature in a child is one of parental actions rather than preaching. Experiencing awe and wonder in nature, hope and trust in neighbors, and care of animals and elders all help children grow on their way to 'authenticity' and fulfillment of their future lives.

A photo of what young ones have done is spiritual indeed.

A Son's Spirit

The chair is empty now.
Sports trophies of childhood glory reduced
to catching dust upon the sill.
The half-filled papers only
but a symbol of a half-grown boy.
He passed so quickly through our home,
did we remember to tell him how much we loved him?
Especially when he delivered newspapers at age 10
or spoke at junior high graduation
or got free tuition at a prestigious college.
He didn't mind his desk was a wobbly table
whereever he was, he showed he was able!

Meditation: Threads of Wisdom

In this meditation we invite you to shape an imaginary quilt made from the threads of events in your life.

Light a candle. Hold a beautiful piece of fabric, a scarf, or small pillow. Relax with music. Settle in a quiet place.

Close your eyes.

Imagine selecting fabric from a baby dress—perhaps toddler best. Let this be the centerpiece of your quilt.

Spirit of the Living Water, I feel the waters of my first bath refreshing every fiber of my being.

Navy gabardine or plaid polyester. A swatch from the skirt I wore the first day of school.

Wisdom of the Living God, I finger the fabric that clothes me *while I grew in your gifts of knowing and becoming.*

There are many pieces to add. Purple satin from my dance costume, the blue felt number 13 on my basketball uniform.

Creator God, these pieces nudge me to remember that recreation is needed to weave a balanced life.

Stitch in memory blocks. A blue jeans pocket when I picked berries, fabric from the boys' cowboy vests and girls' Easter dresses.

Creator of all, I tailor this quilt with reminders of the many ways I have created and supported life.

Great Weaver of the World--with scraps of old, I pattern the new, fingering dreams of long ago, weaving in my hopes that all the pieces of my life will shape the garments of my memories.

Threads of Wisdom

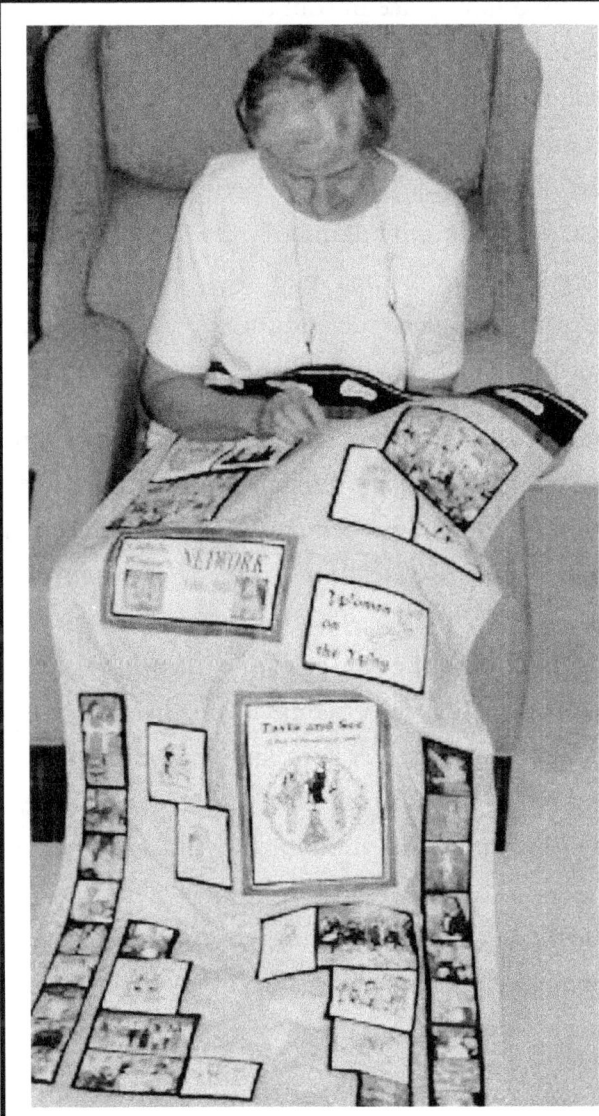

A quilt for comfort
but not for my bed
its silver threads tie
thoughts
in my head.
I sew on a snapshot
when I was in school
or in a workshop
wielding a tool.
Some symbol of
my special days
photo memories
sewed on to stay.

Great joy in my heart
will arrive.
as my past keeps
my present alive!

Women's Circle

We sit in a circle telling stories so dear
but then sad ones with woe would often appear.
How can we grow without depth in our sharing?
Both happy and sad have place in soul bare-ing.
Our circle seemed empty as we started our Way
Our linear brains had nothing to say
but when imaginations filled up the air
then nothingness vanished and was no longer there.
Walking in woodlands and talking to trees
finding a seashell half buried in sand
phantasies came to our rescue and then
enrich our lives like beating the band!

In 1990 I was involved in starting women's spiritual discussion groups. We had simple guidelines that included every woman must talk, keep the confidence of the group, listen to others, be open to all points of view, talk about feelings and reactions, but remember it is not a therapy group to solve problems.

The first topics we discussed were the power of our names, power of our birthplace, where we've lived, and special people in our lives. Some of the activities we used were to discuss ourselves with and without masks we made, playing with black and white colors for sides of our personalities, using rattles or small drums to have fun with, and a talking object to pass to whomever had the floor.

Great discussion can follow talk about sand, feathers, lavender, flowers, jewelry, or candles. When women tell their stories, much of it will be a movement on their own development and authenticity.

> ***God is no White Knight who charges into the world to pluck us like distressed damsels from the jaws of dragons or disease. God chooses to become present to and through us. It is up to us to rescue one another.***
> Nancy Mairs

Women's Circle

My sharing group today with seven wise old gals
talked about the gratefulness we have in being pals.
Nature is a gift for one who soaks it up all days
while three agreed their *spouse* was cause for grateful ways.
Summertime and *water* evoked some joyful praise
and makes us count our blessings and rejoice in many ways
but what keeps us healthy and will save the world from ill
is the *friendship* that we nurture over any kind of pill.

The Woman July 20, 1985
(With meter/rhyme of The Raven by Edgar Allen Poe)

Once upon a summer evening . . . as I sought escape
from grieving over a twist of fate in life I couldn't control
So I sought out Mercy Center . . . searching . . . hoping . . .
seeking ways and means of coping
With nine others I started rapping . . . rapping at my inner door
seeking self as sis and daughter . . . searching parts of self so dusty . . .
finding traits unused and rusty I found this . . . and something more.

As my journey I was tracking . . . in my brain I started racking
tracing my own self in stages . . . back through mem'ry's book of pages
past my birth unto conception . . . to the time of life's inception
I went tapping . . . tapping at my inner door.
Searching parts of self so dusty . . . finding traits unused and rusty
I found this . . . and something more.

Once inside I flung the shutter . . . my heart rising in a flutter
there I found a strange new Woman . . . one unknown to me before
I was like a Goya painting . . . stopped in time . . . new growth a'waitin'
baring self in acts of mourning, weeping, crying tears of mourning
nursing on the strengths of sisters . . . coming through their inner doors
I found this . . . and something more.

So my soul I started purging . . . this new woman came emerging
shaping clay as hands a prayin' . . . feet and legs and voice a 'neighing
weaving webs of yarn in angles . . . woman freed herself of tangles
Elements of earth and fire moved my mind to further knocking
back behind the inner door; my whole ego I was rocking
this I found . . . and something more.

Woman feeling she's a sinner . . . woman born to be a winner
exorcising grief and losings . . . stepping past oppressive use-ings
Anointing self with tears and oil, nourished by another's toil
in each woman there is goddess . . . worker, activist and prophet
So I'm writing, sharing, praying . . . to my Woman I am saying
birth yourself in God's "She" image . . . hide no more 'neath inner door
Answered Woman . . . nevermore!   *Arlene Goetze*

The Woman

Is this what
it's like, God?
On top of the world
beyond the fence
above the stair
holding in space
suspended in air
watching and waiting
secure in my thoughts
serene by myself
alone but not lonely
connected
with you
in my soul?
What a team
we make!

The Holy Oak

The oak tree is one of the most sacred of trees, often called the God Tree. In past centuries it was prized by Celts and Druids as the home of fairies who could give strength and endurance to anyone who was within its aura. It was also associated with gods from many parts of the world. In sacred groves of oaks, a Goddess was believed to impart wisdom.

The Fairy Bible, Teresa Moorey

The oak history has both magic and medicine. When one dreams or rests under an oak tree, it can predict health and long life. Climbing a tree could mean sadness in the future. Catching a fallen leaf brings good luck of not getting a cold in the coming winter.

Natural remedies are many related to the tree bark with its strong astringent properties. It was used internally as a tea to fight diarrhea and externally to heal wounds and eczema. Oak leaves, according to American folk medicine, would cure frostbite.

The Oak tree is believed to boost energy levels and help people achieve goals. The tree has a mirror image . . . its roots below ground mirror the branches above ground.

Oak wood is valuable for furniture. King Arthur's round table was constructed from one cross section of a large oak. Carrying a piece of oak brings good luck to one who carries it.

North America has some 90 species out of the 600 species. It has been used for thousands of years, but a tree must grow 150 years before its wood can be used for construction which includes floors, wine barrels, furniture, and firewood.

urbanara.co.uk

The Holy Oak

The Wye Oak 1500 -2002. • **The Quiet Giant in 1979**
A symbol of time passed and time to come

A memory, just an illusion, this old white oak might say
500 years I've grown in glory, spreading joy in my own way
Glad when children pose beneath me, sad when age attacks my core
When the past exceeds the future, even I can hope for more
More time to comfort weary people, more time to make air you need
Giving shelter, grace, and beauty, that has been my lifelong deed.

The Wye Oak was the largest white oak in the U.S. In 2002 the massive trunk collapsed in a thunderstorm in Maryland. At its end, the tree was 31 feet, 8 inches around, 96 feet tall, and the trunk weighed 61,000 pounds.

Spirit of a Tree

How is your God Tree today? A friend recently told me the story of her God Tree — an apple tree that grew up with her family of four children. She made such delicious pippin apple pies that her kids loved to take them to school even in college. The tree provided shade and swings for grandchildren when they arrived.

The tree was home to a woodpecker and her babies and then a bevy of bees. It was such a blessing that when the tree lost a limb and died, she kept a slice of the trunk for a memoir in her sewing room. It inspires the gorgeous prayer shawls and quilts she makes today.

I was surprised when an intuitive healer who solved some significant health problems in my family, told me to find my own God Tree as part of my healing. That seemed as though it might be taking natural remedies too far, but I decided to find one in the park across the street. I started dowsing all the trees I passed . . . maybe 40 or 50.

Only two trees moved my pendulum to reveal they were God Trees for me. They were next to each other and hovered over the sidewalk where I previously had fallen on the concrete walk but surprisingly didn't break any bones. On my walk these days, I often stop to massage some of the tiny shoots sprouting on these evergreen trees. They give me great spiritual comfort!

Perhaps you can find yourself a God Tree . . . one to talk with, breathe its air, touch new sprouts, and absorb unexpected wisdom.

I found my first God Tree years ago in my back yard, after a graduate school assignment in spirituality gave me that homework. This Mayten tree sheds tiny leaves all year round, and it has been trimmed with branches cut in poor pruning fashion.

It reminds me of God because our idea of God has been altered in many fashions by human tree trimmers down through time. But each of my three God Trees sends me different forms of comfort and hope, even though none of them is an oak tree.

Spirit of a Tree

An all-encompassing umbrella of shade
shielding picnic-ers and lovers
your gnarled fingers branch out
making steps for children on their way to high adventure.
The bite of whizzing blades cuts to your very core
no more a nesting site for birds.
Perhaps a bookcase or a chair, a baby's crib
will keep you holding the precious things in life.
Oh I weep for the glorious gift you were
and try to rejoice for what you may become.

Graceful Art of Dying

Death is often considered a blessing for the old or very sick. Death is usually viewed as cruel for the young or healthy. Yet death comes with warning, on its own time, in its own way . . . but there is one fact we cannot argue . . . death comes.

Our three major Western religions remind us that after death something else comes . . . a type of life or level of consciousness that humans can only envision. No one really knows what lies beyond the grave, but we are learning what happens in the journey we must take to get there.

Since the process of dying is much like birthing, it is helpful to have midwives to usher us through the hard work of leaving our bodies. It is soothing to know we will experience a quality of radiance where our skin becomes so radiant that others can see it in our aura and our eyes.

It is enlightening to know that at times we will appreciate silence and withdrawal as well as movements of the sacred, as we step from earthly consciousness to another level we can only imagine.

Rather than look at death as something negative and depressing, we can see it as a normal stage of growth, of moving from life focused on our body to a new form centered on our soul.

During funeral ceremonies, family members can offer symbols of the one who has died: a tablecloth she embroidered, favorite recipes she cooked, blooms from her garden, a favorite pillow, and photos of her family members.

Persons present can surround and touch the casket and pray

We bless your hair that the wind has played with
We bless your eyes that have looked on us with love
We bless your ears that listened to our voices
We bless your arms that hugged us
We bless your feet that walked your path through life,
May your Spirit now be free!

from Blessing for Dead, Starhawk

Graceful Art

God, I'm still talking
to my husband. The way I used to do,
although its nine years now since he
left home to move upstairs with you.
I know he's dust within this tomb
and that his sprit's free,
but I'm still talking to my husband.
God, give hm a hug for me.

A Spiritual Will

A Spiritual Will is a love letter to be read to your family. It is unique since it reflects the heart and mind of the writer on many occasions. At the end of life, a Spiritual Will can include burial instructions, blessings, and personal or spiritual gifts for the family.

Here are parts of my Will for my Remembrance ceremony:

Dear Family,

You have all read a few of the millions of words I have written for publication during my lifetime but these are just for you.

- Who wants my gift of writing? When I wrote **Our Family History** in 2007, I hoped to find ancestors who were writers or poets but I didn't. Writing did not start with me, but the thank you notes you've written me in verse reveals many of you have writing skills. So please write poems often.

- My 18 drums that I took to nursing homes to energize memory patients I leave to my 18 grandchildren. I know you will honor your elders as you honored me but know that drumming is for health also. Beat your heartbeat to enlarge your love for all living things.

- I leave you each a copy of our family script for our annual production of Gifts for Baby Jesus at Christmas . . . also the scarves worn by shepherds, crowns by 3 Wise Men/Women. Please share this tradition with your offspring. It makes us all laugh so much.

- Each of your families has a singing bowl so chime, and let it sing out healing spiritual energy often to make you feel comfort and hope.

Now I ask you each to light a candle and sing "This little Light of Mine, I'm gonna' let it shine!" Let your flames go out into a world, often dark, and brighten it with love, justice, and joy. I'll be listening and watching . . . so sing loud!

Love mom, grandmom, aunt, cousin, friend S. . .

A Spiritual Will

Grandma Eva always brought a pie
whenever family gathered
She loved to sit and count the kids
that she and hubby fathered
She always found kind things to say
about all folks she knew
She waited tables in a golf club
serving lunch and dinner too.
Now we gather and lay a wreath
as we stand with solemn face
to give her our loving attention
while we sing Amazing Grace?

**God, prod us to give more attention
while our loved ones are still with us.**

Healing Drums

A song can awaken a soul. When we listen to music, we might get goose bumps, breathe more deeply, or feel a flood of emotions that bring us to tears. Old memories might surface. The human response to music is indicative of how deeply it touches the mind, body, heart, and soul. Music can provide the support we need in life's challenging moments, and it can become part of the daily routine for spirituality and health. Enjoy the powerful path of healing—through the power of music.
Joan Borysenko, PhD in Music Medicine, Christine Stevens MSW

Drums were always loud noisemakers I tried to avoid as a child. As a journalist I wrote positive stories about the power of these noisemakers to lower blood pressure, reduce anxiety, and bring calmness into difficult parts of life. In the 1990s, I took workshops in simple ways to drum and minister to people in nursing homes, or how to enliven drum groups to include meditation and drumming ancient rhythms.

At two funeral ceremonies, I gave brief testimonies about how family members could remember their loved ancestors.

Place your hand on your heart, I told them, and do a simple heartbeat as you think of your beloved. At one caregivers' program on happiness, I asked the audience to do this simple act of hand-on-heart for heartbeat. The response was a powerful expression of upbeat energy in a very large church auditorium. People were in tears.

The spirit of that rhythm along with the breathing of the audience was something I hope those caregivers took home to do with those they minister to. It was heaven on earth in my memory list.

Healing Drums

I've got that joy, deep in my heart.
I've got that joy, deep in my heart.
A simple phrase on a buffalo drum
makes dozing elders start to hum.
I am a tower of strength within and without
I am a tower of strength within
The circle of patients in chairs with wheels
begin to wonder just what each feels.
I am full of life. I am full of life.
Tap Tap A boom boom. Tap Tap a boom boom.
One old man throws off his mental haze
Standing up he shouts the phrase.
I am alive. I am alive.

Spirit of Laughter

Laughing Yoga is a combination of combining breathing exercises with laughing. Yoga, from Sanskrit "Yui" means to get hold of, integrate, and harmonize all parts of life. Laughing Yoga with its Laughing Circles uses breathing activities with laughing exercises to relax body and mind. Just as it takes a deep breath, the body is calmed, heart rate slows, and blood gets fresh oxygen. One is aware of the present moment, free of the past and future to 'simply being' in the moment.

laughteronlineuniversity.com

Christians can find great forms of humor and laughter in the Bible. Jesus as a young man turned jugs of water into wine at a wedding. Is that something to laugh at? Sarah heard God tell her she was pregnant at age 90. She named her son Isaac meaning "he laughs."

Rev. James Martin, a Jesuit priest and author of **Between Heaven and Mirth: Why Joy, Humor, and Laughter are at the Heart of Spiritual Life** explains the sacred link between humor and spirituality. Humor is a virtue because it helps us take ourselves lightly, he writes. Laughter is a gift to enjoy God's world. God sent Jesus in human form for human beings to better enter into a spiritual relationship with the Divine.

Laughter is a spiritual release. When people laugh at something ridiculous, it reveals the world is not perfect so if people can laugh at themselves, that is good. It means they can joke and enjoy life. This involves a release of spiritual energy.

It's like saying "I love this life" or "I enjoy this world" or "I'm not so perfect after all." How can we say that each of those insights is not spiritual?

Make a list of joyful and fun things that help you laugh at yourself and your experiences, he suggests.

Spirit of Laughter

Ok God so we're editing
rearranging your creation
shaking sparkles on our eyes
stapling on some curly ties
diamonding our saggy bags
playing in our comfy rags
feathering our facial tones
adding rouge to high cheek bones
polishing some beauty spots
adding glitter lots and lots
as we massage our outer skin,
we're shaping up the soul within.
Bodywork! Soulwork!
Can't have one without the other
and having fun with magic masks
boosts our love for one another.

Spirit of Ancestors

To respect our spiritual ancestors is to know that we don't just come from a lineage of blood but also of ideas. It is to realize that we are continually re-created and helping to re-create anew as we influence each other.
Kat Liu, Unitarian Society

When I published Our Family History in 2009, I hoped to learn careers and health history of my extended family. It never occurred to me then to also search for *spiritual ancestors*. I could deal easily with thousands of photos and seven family trees, but how does one record something or someone that is not visible?

The above quote was found in my computer search for spiritual ancestors, and it suggests our DNA is a lineage of blood while a spiritual lineage is of ideas. This separates us from the physical traits of people on our family tree and ties us to thoughts that affect our spiritual level of growth.

I only met one of my grandparents one day so I do not have spiritual memories of them. The people who move my mind and soul to authenticity are ones I know in my present life.

After a lifetime in one religion, my thinking and wisdom has certainly been developed by priests and nuns as teachers. I have been uplifted and impressed by friends and present relatives—those who have showed me the beauty of exquisite sewing banners for church, of creating humorous cartoons, or just sunning in our source of light.

My spiritual models live around me now as I travel *On my Way.*

Spiritual Ancestors

Dear Grandma
Is this a photo of myself I see
in two frames just before me?
Does my brown hair have DNA you brushed
when you caught chickens on your farm?
Does your finesse in cooking supper
spur my stirring soup from scratch?
Do I love reading because you walked
barefoot many miles just to learn to read?
I hope you find yourself in my mirror
as I reflect your being in the frame!
Love, Your granddaughter

Meditation: Of Silence and Sound

Be Still! Listen!
Be present to your ears tuning them to your heart
 as it pulses God energy through your veins.

Listen to the rhythm of your soul and melody of feelings
 the tempo of your zeal.
Be still and listen to your heart . . . to your soul
 to the very center of yourself.

Silent still sense the swallow in your throat
 the readiness of your voice stilled yet alert . . .
waiting to push the truth of your being into sound.

Be ready to speak noble words and soothing sounds,
 the time for silence is no more.
Give voice to your compassion and compromise
 truthfulness and trust . . . justice and judgment
 loyalty and love.

Whisper of your grace, your elegance and energy
 croon forth your caring and wisdom
 state your strength in no uncertain terms
 preach in protection of your rights
roar out in the wilderness for justice and fair play.

Speak your truth, be silent no more.
Let your voice be an instrument of Divine truth.
Let the voice of your Spirit be heard through you.

On our Way

Shadows and Pillars
I see myself in dark and light
in pillars carved of stone
A mirror image shaped like me
or can it be a clone
We have the same old DNA
it travels through the ages
Our eyes and hair both look alike
no matter what life stages
My time runs out and yours begins
You might write verse like me
You'll add your own distinctive
touch to shape our family tree.

Letter of Goodbye

Dear Readers:

The beginning word often warps into the ending word. Did you see yourself in any of the photos in this book?

Were you curious when you remember your days in a crib protected by bars? What bars today keep you from practicing any virtues in the **Innocent** section? *Is helpfulness* as much as *pleasure* a goal in your life?

Conversation among teens, an **Ordinary** pastime, mentions the importance of listening, respect, and openness to one another as critical to worthwhile conversations regardless of age. Being present in persons to whom we speak can be a spiritual experience, far superior to talking to a person remote on a cell phone.

Can our physical bodies do anything that is not spiritual? Even the simple act of holding **Hands** activates the hormone that makes us feel a part of things. An unknown voice reminds us that touching another has the "complex simplicity of saying so much by doing so little."

Are you a **Pray-er** who has tried clowning around while you pray? Our society has now added Easter bunnies and singing carols at Christmas pageants which add lightness and humor to sacred feasts. Dancing sometimes shows up in churches around altars that create the energy of frolic and fun with the Divine.

How do you **remember** the spiritual highlights in your life? Certainly taking photos is at the top of the list. They can be saved and remembered in a Spiritual Box or a Spiritual Quilt. We are like a Holy Tree that has great value as furniture once it stops giving us oxygen, the very essence of our lives. Our physical lives on earth do carry us into a new spirit life in an unknown realm.

May the words and photos in this book uplift you and be one of the many stones along your pathway . . . be blessed On Your Way!

Arlene Goetze, Photographer, Poet, Writer

Steps to the Future

Six stepping stones around the corner
a journey beckons me
but are they steps to take me forward
or return me where I am?
Are they leading somewhere
in my future
or making memories of now
Should I just stand and meditate
Why do I just hesitate
I know I'm going to celebrate
whatever they create! Amen!

Publications by Arlene Goetze

Wisdom On the Way
Women On the Way
Our Family History
4 Church History Books
      Resurrection in Sunnyvale CA
      St. Joseph in Cupertino
      St. Martin in San Jose
      St. Mary in Los Gatos
2 Diocesan Directories for the Diocese of San Jose CA

89 Issues of *Network for Women's Spirituality*, a newspaper edited by Arlene Goetze and published by Catholic Women's Network 1989-2005 are in the Archives of Santa Clara University and libraries of U. of Notre Dame, U. of Dayton, and Harvard U. Both **'On the Way'** books are in the Archives with **Wisdom on the Way** in the Harvard library.

Arlene was the first female editor of the University of Portland **Beacon in 1955**.

The Author

For half a century, author Arlene Goetze has taken photos at home and work that have been the subject for her writing *Photo Reflections* and publishing them in newspapers, books, and family publications for some 40 years.

She was the first female editor of the student newspaper at the University of Portland in 1955 and started freelancing to national newspapers while raising seven children as a military wife in the 1970s. After establishing Communications for the Diocese of San Jose in 1981-5, she founded Catholic Women's Network, a non-profit educational organization, and edited **Network for Women's Spirituality** in 1989-2005, a newspaper now in the Archives of Santa Clara University for educational purposes on women and spirituality. It is also in libraries of Harvard and U of Notre Dame and Dayton.

Arlene has a B.A. in English/Journalism from the University of Portland in 1956 and M.S. in Spirituality from Santa Clara University, 1994, and is the author of nine books for non-profit groups and churches.

She has been active as a reiki practitioner, spiritual writer and retreat leader, leader of Drumming for Health for elders. and educator of EFT and No Toxins for Children. Her family includes seven children and 18 grandchildren. She and her husband Earl live in Silicon Valley since his military retirement in 1979. *photowrite67@yahoo.com*

www.ingramcontent.com/pod-product-compliance
Lightning Source LLC
Chambersburg PA
CBHW060306010526
44108CB00041B/2558